D1611321

Table of Contents

Christmas

Kwanzaa

Editor	JUDY CROW
Assistant Editors	SHIRLEY PATRICK
	KRIS KIRST
Book Design	GREG SMITH
Production Artist	DEBBY KEEL
Photography Supervisor	SCOTT CAMPBELL
Photographer	ANDY J. BURNFIELD
Photo Stylist	MARTHA COQUAT
Photo Assistant	CRYSTAL KEY

Chief Executive Officer	JOHN ROBINSON
Publishing Marketing Director	DAVID MCKEE
Product Development Director	VIVIAN ROTHE
Product Development Manager	CONNIE ELLISON
Publishing Services Manager	ANGE VAN ARMAN

Customer Service 1-800-449-0440
Pattern Services (903) 636-5140

CREDITS
Sincerest thanks to all the designers,
manufacturers and other professionals
whose dedication has made this book possible.

Special thanks to
Quebecor Printing Book Group, Kingsport, Tenn.

Copyright © 2002 The Needlecraft Shop
All rights reserved. No part of this book may be
reproduced in any form or by any means without the
written permission of the publisher, excepting
brief quotations in connection with reviews written
specifically for inclusion in magazines,
newspapers and other publications.

Library of Congress Cataloging-in-Publication Data
ISBN: 1-57367-122-3
First Printing: 2002
Library of Congress Catalog Card Number: 2002104513
Published and Distributed by
The Needlecraft Shop, Big Sandy, Texas 75755
Printed in the United States of America.

Visit us at
NeedlecraftShop.com

Dear Friends

I grew up in a small town where everyone knew everyone else. Anytime a town event took place it became a great social gathering; you could count on young and old turning out. Parades were such an event. They never lasted more than 10 minutes but would showcase our local high school band, cheerleaders and floats representing the two civic clubs in town. Last, but certainly not least, was the fire truck featuring Cinders the firehouse dog—he was actually a basset hound!

The Fourth of July was always my favorite holiday. Not only did we have a parade in the morning, but starting at noon, we would have a picnic at the city park. After lunch there were games and competition for the kids and the older men set up card tables under the trees for an afternoon of forty-two. Of course the whole day of celebration ended with a gigantic display of fireworks.

I remember my grandmother and other ladies in the community setting up their quilting frames or bringing out various types of needlework at these events. I can still see Granny Bee, a wonderful lady in town who had no family but everyone called her Granny. Her hair in a knot on the top of her head, her shawl around her shoulders and her hands shaking, she stitched cross bookmarks made from plastic canvas, which she gave to everyone at church on Christmas Eve.

Perhaps this is where my love for needlework began. To me, holidays and homemade gifts go hand in hand. I can't imagine a holiday going by that I don't give or receive something that is homemade. This book is full of wonderful holiday and gift ideas. I hope you enjoy your Holidays on Parade.

Judy Crow

Happy New Year!

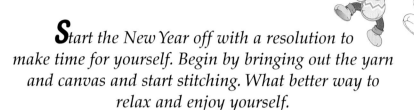

*S*tart the New Year off with a resolution to make time for yourself. Begin by bringing out the yarn and canvas and start stitching. What better way to relax and enjoy yourself.

New Year's Baby

Designed by Eunice Asberry

Celebrate new beginnings with friends, family and this New Year's Baby!

SIZE: 5¼" x 10" [13.3cm x 25.4cm]

SKILL LEVEL: Average

MATERIALS:
• One sheet of 7-mesh plastic canvas
• Four ¾" [19mm] brads
• Worsted-weight or plastic canvas yarn
  (for amounts see Color Key)

CUTTING INSTRUCTIONS:
A: For Body, cut one according to graph.
B: For Arms, cut two according to graph.
C: For Legs, cut two according to graph.
D: For Banner, cut one according to graph.

STITCHING INSTRUCTIONS:
1: Using colors indicated and continental stitch, work pieces according to graphs; omitting attachment areas, with matching colors, overcast edges of pieces.

2: Using colors (Separate into individual plies, if desired.) and embroidery stitches indicated, embroider detail on A and D pieces as indicated on graphs. With white, whipstitch D to right side of A as indicated.

3: Inserting brads through indicated ◆ holes, assemble A-C pieces together as shown in photo.

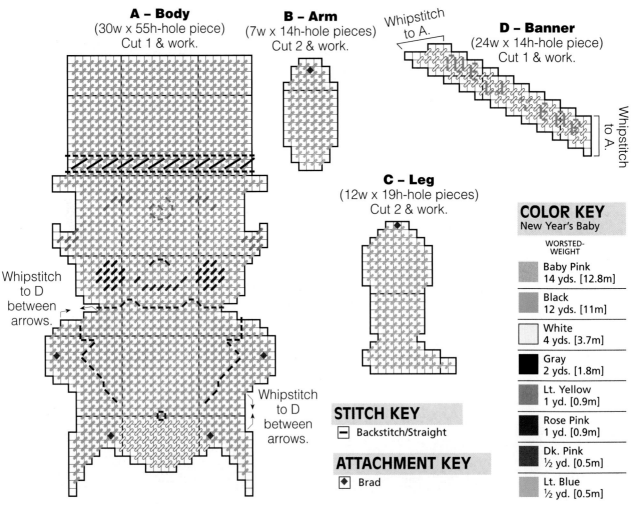

A – Body
(30w x 55h-hole piece)
Cut 1 & work.

B – Arm
(7w x 14h-hole pieces)
Cut 2 & work.

Whipstitch to A.

D – Banner
(24w x 14h-hole piece)
Cut 1 & work.

Whipstitch to A.

Whipstitch to D between arrows.

Whipstitch to D between arrows.

C – Leg
(12w x 19h-hole pieces)
Cut 2 & work.

COLOR KEY
New Year's Baby

WORSTED-WEIGHT

	Baby Pink	14 yds. [12.8m]
	Black	12 yds. [11m]
	White	4 yds. [3.7m]
	Gray	2 yds. [1.8m]
	Lt. Yellow	1 yd. [0.9m]
	Rose Pink	1 yd. [0.9m]
	Dk. Pink	½ yd. [0.5m]
	Lt. Blue	½ yd. [0.5m]

STITCH KEY
− Backstitch/Straight

ATTACHMENT KEY
◆ Brad

Valentine's Day!

Express your love for stitching as well as for that special person by creating a heartfelt Valentine's gift in plastic canvas.

Bear Candy Dish

Designed by Christina Laws

Let your Valentine know how "beary" special they are by presenting them with a dish filled with candy.

SIZE: 7½" x 7½" x 7¾" [19cm x 19cm x 19.7cm]

SKILL LEVEL: Average

MATERIALS:
- Two sheets of 7-mesh plastic canvas;
- Craft glue or glue gun;
- Worsted-weight or plastic canvas yarn (for amounts see Color Key)

CUTTING INSTRUCTIONS:
A: For Bear Front, cut one according to graph.
B: For Bear Back, cut one according to graph.
C: For Base Top, cut one according to graph.
D: For Base Sides, cut four 21w x 12h-holes (no graph).
E: For Dish Sides, cut four 49w x 13h-holes.
F: For Dish Bottom, cut one 49w x 49h-holes.

STITCHING INSTRUCTIONS:
NOTE: F is not worked.

1: Using colors and stitches indicated, work A-C and E pieces according to graphs; work D pieces using red and continental stitch.

2: Using black (Separate into individual plies, if desired.) and embroidery stitches indicated, embroider detail on A and B pieces as indicated on graphs.

3: For Bear, with tan for tabs and with matching colors as shown in photo, whipstitch A and B pieces wrong sides together.

4: For Base, with red, whipstitch C and D pieces wrong sides together as indicated; whipstitch Base to F as indicated. Insert tabs of Bear into cutouts on Base Top; glue to secure.

5: For Dish, with white, whipstitch short edges of E pieces wrong sides together and to F as indicated; overcast unfinished top edges.

STITCH KEY
- ⊟ Backstitch/Straight

ATTACHMENT KEY
- ☐ Base/Dish Bottom

COLOR KEY
Bear Candy Dish

WORSTED-WEIGHT

■	Red 35 yds. [32m]
▨	White 15 yds. [13.7m]
▨	Brown 12 yds. [11m]
▨	Tan 3 yds. [2.7m]
■	Black 2 yds. [1.8m]

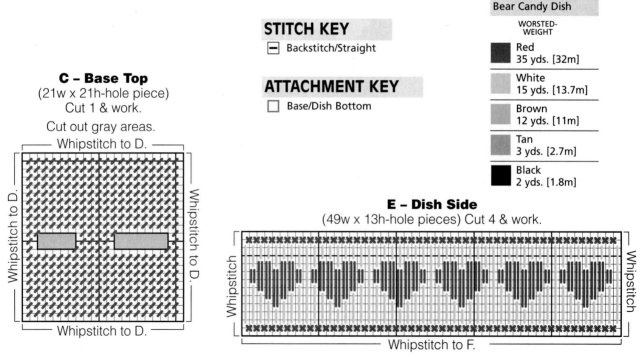

C – Base Top
(21w x 21h-hole piece)
Cut 1 & work.
Cut out gray areas.

Whipstitch to D.
Whipstitch to D.
Whipstitch to D.
Whipstitch to D.

E – Dish Side
(49w x 13h-hole pieces) Cut 4 & work.

Whipstitch
Whipstitch
Whipstitch to F.

A – Bear Front
(30w x 50h-hole piece)
Cut 1 & work, leaving uncoded
areas unworked.

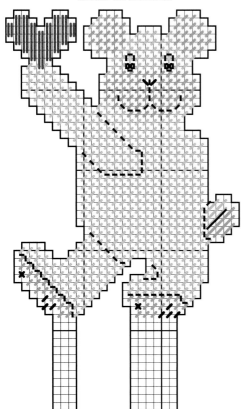

B – Bear Back
(30w x 50h-hole piece)
Cut 1 & work, leaving uncoded
areas unworked.

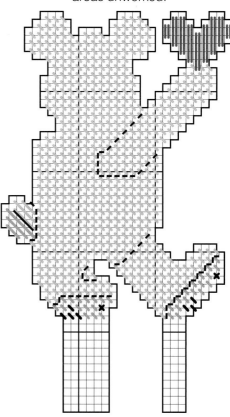

F – Dish Bottom
(49w x 49h-hole piece) Cut 1 & leave unworked.

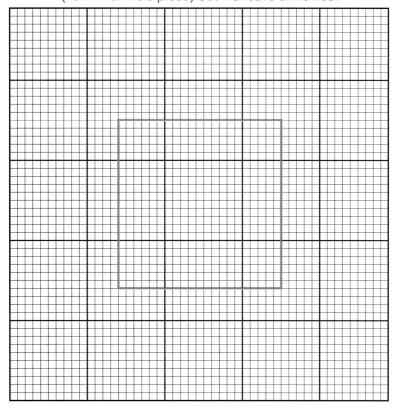

Love Blocks
& Tissue Cover

Designed by Angie Arickx

Express your sentiments for the holiday with matching blocks and tissue cover.

SIZES: Each Block is 3" x 3" x 3" [7.6cm x 7.6cm x 7.6cm]; Tissue Cover loosely covers a 4⅝" x 9⅜" x 3¼" tall [11.7cm x 23.8cm x 8.3cm] tissue box

SKILL LEVEL: Average

MATERIALS:
• Five sheets of 7-mesh plastic canvas
• Velcro® closure (optional)
• Craft glue or glue gun
• Worsted-weight or plastic canvas yarn (for amounts see Color Key)

CUTTING INSTRUCTIONS:
A: For "L", "O", "V" and "E" Block Sides, cut six each 19w x 19h-holes.
B: For Tissue Cover Top, cut one according to graph.
C: For Tissue Cover Sides, cut two 65w x 23h-holes.
D: For Tissue Cover Ends, cut two 33w x 23h-holes.

E: For Optional Cover Bottom and Flap, cut one for Bottom 65w x 33h-holes and one for Flap 65w x 12h-holes (no graphs).

STITCHING INSTRUCTIONS:
NOTE: E pieces are not worked.

1: Using colors and stitches indicated, work A-D pieces according to graphs; with pink, overcast cutout edges of B.

2: For each letter Block (make 4), with lavender, whipstitch matching letter Block A pieces wrong sides together.

3: With pink, whipstitch B-D pieces wrong sides together, forming Cover. For Optional Bottom, whipstitch E pieces together and to one Cover Side according to Optional Tissue Cover Bottom Assembly Illustration; overcast unfinished edges. Glue closure to Flap and inside of Cover (see illustration).

C – Tissue Cover Side
(65w x 23h-hole pieces) Cut 2 & work.

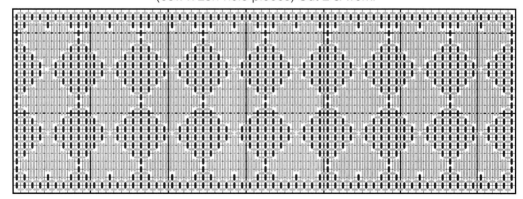

Optional Tissue Cover Bottom Assembly Illustration

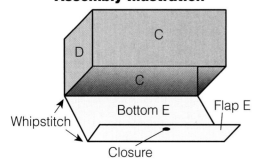

COLOR KEY		
Love Blocks & Tissue Cover		
	WORSTED-WEIGHT	NEED-LOFT®
Pink 4 oz. [113.4g]		#07
Lavender 3½ oz. [99.2g]		#05
White 24 yds. [21.9m]		#41

A – "L" Block Side
(19w x 19h-hole pieces)
Cut 6 & work.

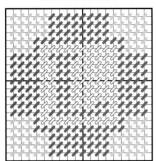

A – "O" Block Side
(19w x 19h-hole pieces)
Cut 6 & work.

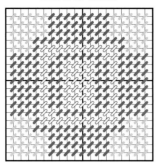

A – "V" Block Side
(19w x 19h-hole pieces)
Cut 6 & work.

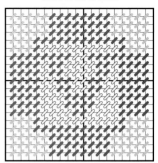

A – "E" Block Side
(19w x 19h-hole pieces)
Cut 6 & work.

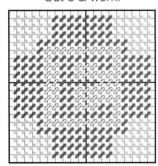

COLOR KEY
Love Blocks & Tissue Cover

	WORSTED-WEIGHT	NEED-LOFT®
Pink	4 oz. [113.4g]	#07
Lavender	3½ oz. [99.2g]	#05
White	24 yds. [22m]	#41

D – Tissue Cover End
(33w x 23h-hole pieces) Cut 2 & work.

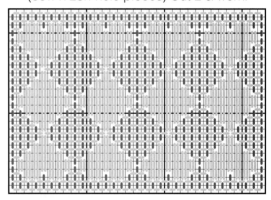

B – Tissue Cover Top
(65w x 33h-hole piece)
Cut 1 & work.

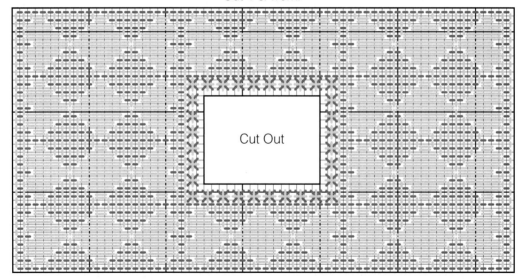

Cut Out

Valentine Mobile

Designed by Nancy Knapp

Hearts abound when you create this great holiday mobile.

SIZE: 9" across x about 30" tall [22.9cm x 76.2cm]

SKILL LEVEL: Challenging

MATERIALS:
- Two sheets of 7-mesh plastic canvas
- One 9" [22.9cm] and one 2½" [6.4cm] metal ring
- 9 yds. [8.2m] of white ¼" [6mm] satin ribbon
- 1¼ yds. [1.1m] of pink 2mm pearl strand
- 1¼ yds. [1.1m] of white 4mm pearl strand
- Four 7mm pearl beads
- Twelve pink ¾" [19mm] silk rosebuds with leaves
- 3½"-long [8.9cm] tapestry needle
- Craft glue or glue gun
- Pearlized metallic cord (for amount see Color Key)
- Worsted-weight or plastic canvas yarn (for amounts see Color Key)

CUTTING INSTRUCTIONS:
A: For Hearts #1, cut six according to graph.
B: For Hearts #2, cut six according to graph.
C: For Hearts #3, cut fourteen according to graph.
D: For Hearts #4, cut two according to graph.

STITCHING INSTRUCTIONS:
1: Using colors indicated and continental stitch, work pieces according to graphs.

2: For Hearts #1 (make 3), with country red, whipstitch two A pieces wrong sides together; for Hearts #2 (make 3), with medium rose, whipstitch two B pieces wrong sides together. For Hearts #3 (make 7), with medium rose, whipstitch two C pieces wrong sides together; for Heart #4, with cord, whipstitch cutout and outer edges of D pieces wrong sides together.

NOTES: Cut fourteen 9" [22.9cm] lengths of ribbon; tie each length into a bow.
Cut fourteen 3" [7.6cm] lengths of pink pearls and three 12" [30.5cm] lengths of white pearls.

3: Glue two rosebuds and one length of white pearls around outer edge of each side of each Heart #1 as shown in photo. Glue one bow and one length of pink pearls to each side of each Heart #3 as shown.

NOTES: Cut remaining ribbon into four 1 yd. [0.9m] lengths and three 9" [22.9cm] lengths; tie each 9" length into a bow.

4: Assemble Hearts, metal rings, ribbon and beads according to Mobile Assembly Diagram; glue bows to outer streamers at ring (see photo).

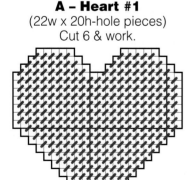

A – Heart #1
(22w x 20h-hole pieces)
Cut 6 & work.

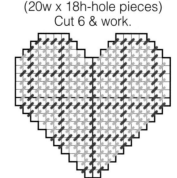

B – Heart #2
(20w x 18h-hole pieces)
Cut 6 & work.

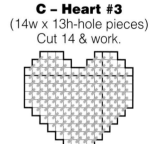

C – Heart #3
(14w x 13h-hole pieces)
Cut 14 & work.

D – Heart #4
(26w x 24h-hole pieces)
Cut 2 & work.

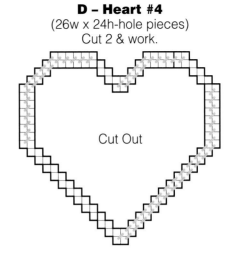

Cut Out

COLOR KEY
Valentine Mobile

	PEARLIZED METALLIC CORD	DARICE®
▨	White 9 yds. [8.2m]	#01

	WORSTED WEIGHT
■	Country Red 60 yds. [54.9m]
▨	Med. Rose 60 yds. [54.9m]

Mobile Assembly Diagram
(Pieces are shown in different colors for contrast.)

Step 1:
Tie one end of each 1 yd. length of ribbon to 2¹/₂" metal ring.

Step 2:
For outer streamers, wrap three of the 1 yd. lengths of ribbon around 9" ring at equal distance from 2¹/₂" ring.

Step 3:
For each streamer, thread one ribbon through needle; working from top to bottom in order shown, insert needle through center of hearts, spacing as indicated, and then through bead.

Step 4:
Tie a knot below each bead to secure; trim ends.

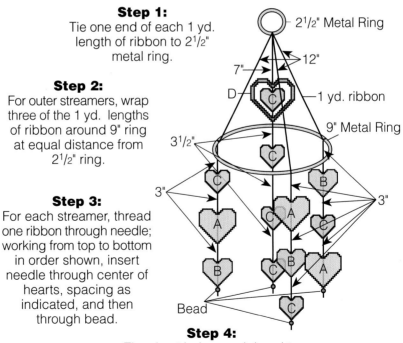

Honeybee Coasters

Designed by Christina Laws

This adorable coaster set is sure to please your honey!

SIZES: Each Coaster is 5½" x 6" [14cm x 15.2cm]; Holder is 2¼" x 4¼" x 2⅜" tall [5.7cm x 10.8cm x 6cm]

SKILL LEVEL: Average

MATERIALS:
• Three sheets of 7-mesh plastic canvas
• Worsted-weight or plastic canvas yarn (for amounts see Color Key)

CUTTING INSTRUCTIONS:
A: For Coaster Fronts and Backings, cut eight (four for Fronts and four for Backings) according to graph.
B: For Holder Sides, cut two according to graph.
C: For Holder Ends, cut two according to graph.
D: For Holder Bottom, cut one 28w x 14h-holes (no graph).

STITCHING INSTRUCTIONS:
NOTE: D and Backing A pieces are not worked.

1: Using colors and stitches indicated, work Front A, B and C pieces according to graphs.

2: Using colors (Separate into individual plies, if desired.) and embroidery stitches indicated, embroider detail on Front A and B pieces as indicated on graphs.

3: For each Coaster (make 4), holding one Backing A to wrong side of one Front A, with matching colors, whipstitch together.

4: For Holder, with red, whipstitch B-D pieces together as indicated and according to Holder Assembly Illustration; overcast unfinished edges.

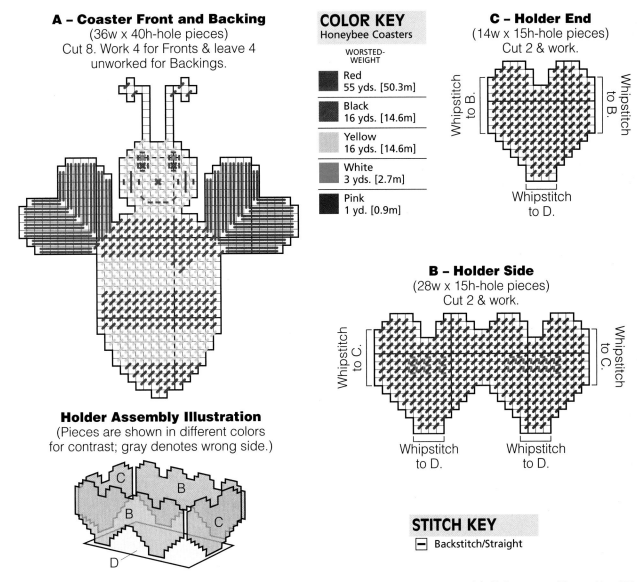

A – Coaster Front and Backing
(36w x 40h-hole pieces)
Cut 8. Work 4 for Fronts & leave 4 unworked for Backings.

COLOR KEY
Honeybee Coasters

WORSTED-WEIGHT

■	Red	55 yds. [50.3m]
■	Black	16 yds. [14.6m]
▨	Yellow	16 yds. [14.6m]
▨	White	3 yds. [2.7m]
■	Pink	1 yd. [0.9m]

C – Holder End
(14w x 15h-hole pieces)
Cut 2 & work.

Whipstitch to B.

Whipstitch to B.

Whipstitch to D.

B – Holder Side
(28w x 15h-hole pieces)
Cut 2 & work.

Whipstitch to C.

Whipstitch to C.

Whipstitch to D.

Whipstitch to D.

Holder Assembly Illustration
(Pieces are shown in different colors for contrast; gray denotes wrong side.)

STITCH KEY
⊟ Backstitch/Straight

Heart Sachet

Designed by Kathy Wirth

This will make a perfect gift for a beloved friend on Valentine's Day.

SIZE: 3½" x 3½" x 1¼" [8.9cm x 8.9cm x 3.2cm], not including tassel or hanger

SKILL LEVEL: Challenging

MATERIALS:
- One sheet of white 10-mesh plastic canvas
- 3" [7.6cm] metallic silver tassel
- 1 yd. [0.9m] white ⅛" [3mm] satin ribbon
- Sixteen crystal E beads
- ½ yd. [0.5m] very fine beading wire
- 9" [22.9cm] square piece of white tulle
- Small amount of potpourri
- ¹⁄₁₆" [2mm] metallic ribbon (for amount see Color Key)
- No. 3 pearl cotton (for amount see Color Key)

CUTTING INSTRUCTIONS:
For Sachet, cut one according to graph.

STITCHING INSTRUCTIONS:
1: Using colors and stitches indicated and leaving uncoded areas unworked, work Sachet according to graph; using metallic ribbon and straight stitch, embroider detail on Sachet as indicated on graph.

2: Using beading wire, attach beads to right side of Sachet as indicated on graph.

3: Place potpourri in center of tulle square; fold tulle over potpourri and tack, forming 3" [7.6cm] square packet.

NOTE: Cut three 12" [30.5cm] lengths of ribbon.

4: Center potpourri packet on wrong side of Sachet; bring two opposite corners together over top of packet. Thread one end of one length of ribbon from back to front through one ◆ hole on corner and remaining end of same ribbon from back to front through ◆ hole on opposite corner; tie into a bow. Repeat with remaining two corners and one 12" ribbon.

5: Tack tassel to one corner of Sachet as shown in photo. For hanger, tie remaining length of ribbon to corner opposite tassel (see photo).

Sachet
(73w x 73h-hole piece)
Cut 1 & work.

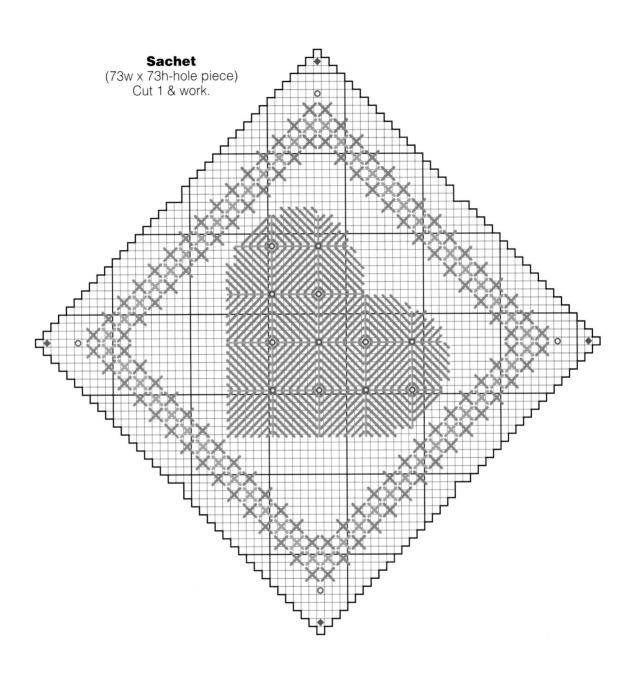

COLOR KEY
Heart Sachet

	¹/₁₆" METALLIC RIBBON	KREINIK
	Silver 6 yds. [5.5m]	#001HL

	NO. 3 PEARL COTTON	ANCHOR
	Med. Antique Rose 12 yds. [11m]	#07

STITCH KEY
⊟ Straight

ATTACHMENT KEY
◎ Bead
◈ Ribbon

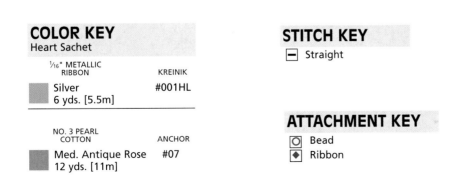

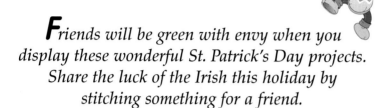

St. Patrick's Day!

***F**riends will be green with envy when you display these wonderful St. Patrick's Day projects. Share the luck of the Irish this holiday by stitching something for a friend.*

Leprechaun Tissue Cover

Designed by Nancy Dorman

Add a touch of green to your home or office with this seasonal tissue box cover.

SIZE: Loosely covers a boutique-style tissue box

SKILL LEVEL: Challenging

MATERIALS:
- 1½ sheets of 10-mesh plastic canvas
- One small package gold confetti
- Craft glue or glue gun
- Medium metallic ribbon (for amount see Color Key)
- Six-strand embroidery floss (for amounts see Color Key)
- Sport-weight yarn (for amounts see Color Key)

CUTTING INSTRUCTIONS:
A: For Sides, cut four 45w x 57h-holes.
B: For Top, cut one according to graph.

C: For Shamrocks, cut twelve according to graph

STITCHING INSTRUCTIONS:
1: Using colors and stitches indicated, work pieces according to graphs; using holly, overcast edges of C pieces. Using holly and herringbone overcast (see stitch illustration on page 22) overcast cutout edges of B.

2: Using braid and three strands floss in colors and embroidery stitches indicated, embroider detail on A pieces as indicated on graph.

3: Using holly and herringbone whipstitch (see stitch illustration), whipstitch A and B pieces wrong sides together, forming Cover; with herringbone overcast, overcast unfinished bottom edges.

4: Glue three Shamrocks and confetti to each Cover Side as shown in photo or as desired.

B – Top
(45w x 45h-hole piece)
Cut 1 & work, filling in uncoded areas using white & continental stitch.

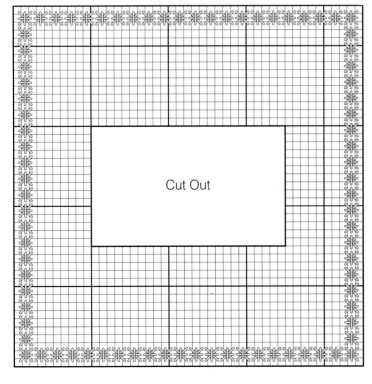

Cut Out

COLOR KEY
Leprechaun Tissue Cover

METALLIC RIBBON		SPORT-WEIGHT	
Gold 4 yds. [3.7m]		Holly 2½ oz. [70.9g]	
EMBROIDERY FLOSS		White 2½ oz. [70.9g]	
Black 1 yd. [0.9m]		Black 50 yds. [45.7m]	
Blue 1 yd. [0.9m]		Rust 6 yds. [5.5m]	
Pink 1 yd. [0.9m]		Flesh Tone 4 yds. [3.7m]	

A – Side
(45w x 57h-hole pieces)
Cut 4 & work, filling in uncoded areas using
white & continental stitch.

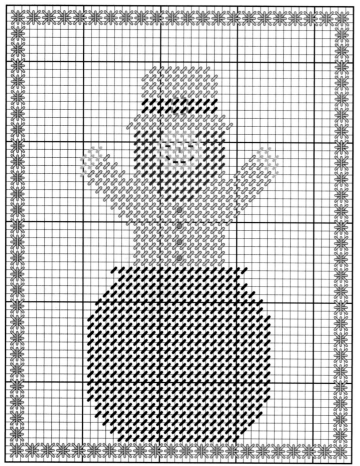

COLOR KEY
Leprechaun Tissue Cover

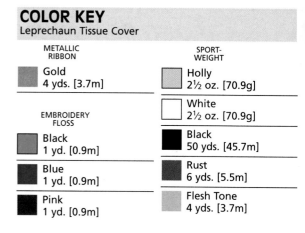

METALLIC RIBBON		SPORT-WEIGHT	
■ Gold 4 yds. [3.7m]		▨ Holly 2½ oz. [70.9g]	
EMBROIDERY FLOSS		□ White 2½ oz. [70.9g]	
■ Black 1 yd. [0.9m]		■ Black 50 yds. [45.7m]	
■ Blue 1 yd. [0.9m]		■ Rust 6 yds. [5.5m]	
■ Pink 1 yd. [0.9m]		▨ Flesh Tone 4 yds. [3.7m]	

Herringbone Overcast Stitch Illustration

Herringbone Whipstitch Stitch Illustration

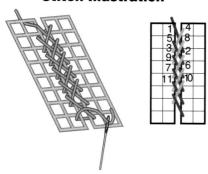

STITCH KEY
⊟ Backstitch/Straight
⊡ French Knot

C – Shamrock
(5w x 5h-hole pieces)
Cut 12 & work.

Cut around
bar
carefully.

Coasters & Mug Insert

Designed by Judy Collishaw & Ruby Thacker

Complete your table setting with these festive leprechaun designs.

SIZES: Each Coaster is 3¾" x 3¾" [9.5cm x 9.5cm]; Coaster Holder is 2¼" x 5" x 4¼" tall [5.7cm x 12.7cm x 10.8cm]; Mug Insert fits inside a 4"-tall [10.2cm] plastic snap-together mug

SKILL LEVEL: Average

MATERIALS:
- 1½ sheets of 7-mesh plastic canvas
- One white plastic snap-together mug
- Craft glue or glue gun
- Heavy metallic braid (for amount see Coasters Color Key)
- No. 5 pearl cotton (coton perle) (for amounts see Coasters Color Key)
- Metallic cord (for amount, see Mug Insert Color Key)
- Worsted-weight or plastic canvas yarn (for amounts see individual Color Keys)

CUTTING INSTRUCTIONS:
A: For Coasters, cut four 24w x 24h-holes.
B: For Holder Sides, cut two according to graph.
C: For Holder Ends, cut two 7w x 22h-holes.

D: For Holder Bottom, cut one 34w x 15h-holes.
E: For Clovers, cut four according to graph.
F: For Mug Insert, cut one 64w x 23h-holes.

STITCHING INSTRUCTIONS:
1: Omitting attachment areas, using colors and stitches indicated, work pieces according to graphs; omitting attachment edges, with forest green for A and D pieces and with matching colors, overcast A-F pieces.

2: Using pearl cotton and embroidery stitches indicated, embroider detail on A pieces as indicated on graph.

3: For Coaster Holder, with white, whipstitch B-D pieces together as indicated and according to Holder Assembly Illustration. Glue two Clovers to each Holder Side.

4: For Mug Insert, with white, whipstitch short edges of F wrong sides together as indicated. Place Insert in mug and assemble according to manufacturer's instructions.

COLOR KEY
Mug Insert

	METALLIC CORD	NEED LOFT®
	Gold 1½ yd. [1.4m]	#20

	WORSTED WEIGHT	NEED LOFT®
	White 25 yds. [22.9m]	#41
	Christmas Green #28 5 yds. [4.6m]	

F – Mug Insert
(64w x 23h-hole piece) Cut 1 & work.

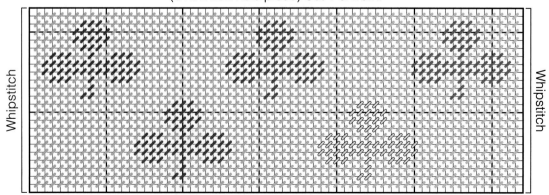

A – Coaster
(24w x 24h-hole pieces)
Cut 4 & work.

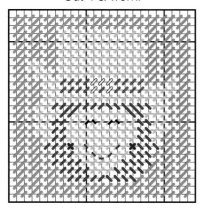

COLOR KEY
Coasters

	METALLIC BRAID KREINIK			WORSTED-WEIGHT	
	Gold #002HL 1 yd. [0.9m]			White 18 yds. [16.5m]	
				Apple Green 12 yds. [11m]	
	NO. 5 PEARL COTTON DMC®			Forest 10 yds. [9.1m]	
	Black #310 1 yd. [0.9m]			Peach 8 yds. [7.3m]	
	Red #321 1 yd. [0.9m]			Rust 8 yds. [7.3m]	
	WORSTED-WEIGHT			Black 2 yds. [1.8m]	
	Kelly Green 40 yds. [36.6m]			Rose 1 yd. [0.9m]	

ATTACHMENT KEY

☐ Holder Side/Holder Bottom

D – Holder Bottom
(34w x 15h-hole piece)
Cut 1 & work.

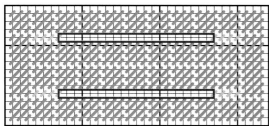

E – Clover
(7w x 7h-hole pieces)
Cut 4 & work.

STITCH KEY

⊟ Backstitch/Straight

B – Holder Side
(26w x 25h-hole pieces)
Cut 2 & work.

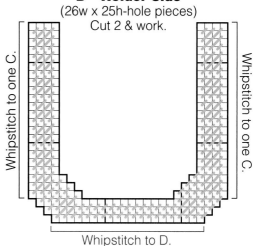

Whipstitch to one C.

Whipstitch to one C.

Whipstitch to D.

C – Holder End
(7w x 22h-hole pieces)
Cut 2 & work.

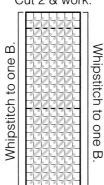

Whipstitch to one B.

Whipstitch to one B.

Coaster Holder Assembly Illustration
(Pieces are shown in different colors for contrast; gray denotes wrong side.)

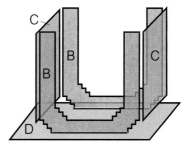

Leprechaun Corner Sitter

Designed by Lynne Langer

This whimsical fellow wants to bring you good luck this St. Paddy's Day.

SIZE: ⅜" x 9" x 10¾" [1cm x 22.9cm x 27.3cm]

SKILL LEVEL: Easy

MATERIALS:
- One sheet of 7-mesh plastic canvas
- Metallic cord (for amount see Color Key)
- Worsted-weight or plastic canvas yarn
  (for amounts see Color Key)

CUTTING INSTRUCTIONS:
A: For Leprechaun, cut one according to graph.
B: For Pot of Gold, cut one according to graph.
C: For Balance Piece #1, cut one 41w x 2h-holes (no graph).
D: For Balance Piece #2, cut one 13w x 2h-holes (no graph).

STITCHING INSTRUCTIONS:
NOTE: C and D pieces are not worked.

1: Using colors and stitches indicated, work A and B pieces according to graphs; omitting attachment areas, with black for Pot of Gold and with matching colors, overcast edges of A and B pieces.

2: Using colors (Separate into individual plies, if desired.) and embroidery stitches indicated, embroider detail on A as indicated on graph.

3: With bright green, whipstitch C and D pieces together at one short edge; whipstitch long edges to A as indicated.

NOTE: Cut one 3" [7.6cm] length of metallic cord.

4: Insert one end of cord from front to back through ◆ hole on A; tie end into a knot to secure. Insert remaining end from front to back through ◆ hole on B; tie end into a knot to secure; trim ends.

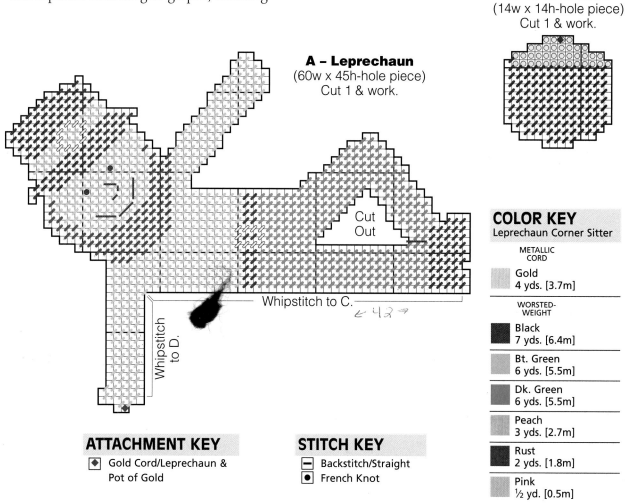

A – Leprechaun
(60w x 45h-hole piece)
Cut 1 & work.

B – Pot of Gold
(14w x 14h-hole piece)
Cut 1 & work.

Cut Out

Whipstitch to C.

Whipstitch to D.

ATTACHMENT KEY
◆ Gold Cord/Leprechaun & Pot of Gold

STITCH KEY
– Backstitch/Straight
● French Knot

COLOR KEY
Leprechaun Corner Sitter

METALLIC CORD
Gold 4 yds. [3.7m]

WORSTED-WEIGHT
Black 7 yds. [6.4m]
Bt. Green 6 yds. [5.5m]
Dk. Green 6 yds. [5.5m]
Peach 3 yds. [2.7m]
Rust 2 yds. [1.8m]
Pink ½ yd. [0.5m]

Leprechaun

Designed by Eunice Asberry

Bring a wee bit o' luck into your home with this smiling elf of Irish folklore.

SIZE: 6¼" x 11¾" [15.9cm x 29.8cm]

SKILL LEVEL: Average

MATERIALS:
- One sheet of 7-mesh plastic canvas
- Four ¾" [19mm] brads
- Worsted-weight or plastic canvas yarn
  (for amounts see Color Key)

CUTTING INSTRUCTIONS:
A: For Body, cut one according to graph.
B: For Arms #1 and #2, cut one each according to graphs.
C: For Legs, cut two according to graph.

STITCHING INSTRUCTIONS:
1: Using colors indicated and continental stitch, work pieces according to graphs; with matching colors, overcast edges of pieces.

2: Using colors and embroidery stitches indicated, embroider detail on A and C pieces as indicated on graphs.

3: Inserting brads through indicated ◆ holes, assemble A-C pieces as shown in photo. Hang as desired.

COLOR KEY
Leprechaun

	WORSTED-WEIGHT
	Lt. Green 27 yds. [24.7m]
	Green 12 yds. [11m]
	Orange 10 yds. [9.1m]
	Flesh Tone 8 yd. [7.3m]
	Black 7 yds. [6.4m]
	Dk. Pink ½ yd. [0.5m]
	Lt. Pink ½ yd. [0.5m]
	Yellow ½ yd. [0.5m]

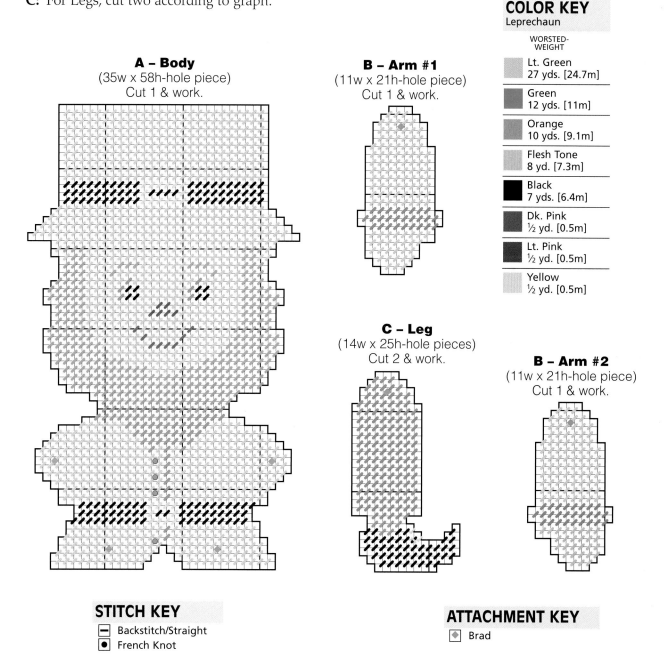

A – Body
(35w x 58h-hole piece)
Cut 1 & work.

B – Arm #1
(11w x 21h-hole piece)
Cut 1 & work.

C – Leg
(14w x 25h-hole pieces)
Cut 2 & work.

B – Arm #2
(11w x 21h-hole piece)
Cut 1 & work.

STITCH KEY
- — Backstitch/Straight
- ● French Knot

ATTACHMENT KEY
- ◆ Brad

Happy Easter!

*You can help the Easter Bunny by stitching
these great projects that will delight children of all ages.
Give as gifts or use as decorations year after year.*

Eggs & Bunny Basket

Designed by Janna Britton

This basket filled with goodies will make a great centerpiece.

SIZE: 9½" across x 8¾" tall [24.1cm x 22.2cm]

SKILL LEVEL: Challenging

MATERIALS:
- Three sheets of 7-mesh plastic canvas
- One 9" [22.9cm] round plastic canvas circle
- One 9" x 12" [22.9cm x 30.5cm] sheet of white felt
- Polyester fiberfill
- Craft glue or glue gun
- Six-strand embroidery floss (for amount see Color Key)
- Worsted-weight or plastic canvas yarn (for amounts see Color Key)

CUTTING INSTRUCTIONS:
A: For Eggs #1-#8 Fronts and Backings, cut two each (one for Front and one for Backing) according to graphs.
B: For Bunny Body, cut one according to graph.
C: For Bunny Arms, cut one according to graph.
D: For Basket Back, cut one according to graph.
E: For Basket Front, cut one according to graph.
F: For Bottom, use 9" circle (no graph).

STITCHING INSTRUCTIONS:
NOTE: F and Backing A pieces are not worked.

1: Using colors and stitches indicated, work Front A and B-E pieces according to graphs; omitting attachment edges, with matching colors as shown in photo, overcast edges of B-E pieces.

NOTE: Using B as a pattern, cut one from felt ⅛" [3mm] smaller at all edges.

2: Using six strands floss and embroidery stitches indicated, embroider eyes on B as indicated on graph. With white, whipstitch wrong side of C to right side of B as indicated; glue felt to wrong side of Bunny Body.

NOTE: Cut six 1" [2.5cm] lengths of fern.

3: For Bunny's Basket, with bright blue, whipstitch wrong side of E to right side of D as indicated; glue or tack basket to center of Bunny Arms as shown in photo. Place cut strands in Basket and glue to secure (see photo).

4: Omitting attachment areas, with pink for A#2, bright blue for A#3 and A#7, yellow for A#4 and A#8, tangerine for A#1 and A#5, and fern for A#6, whipstitch one Backing A to wrong side of

A – Egg #1 Front and Backing
(22w x 29h-hole pieces)
Cut 2; work 1 for Front & leave
1 unworked for Backing.

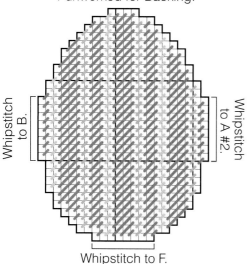

Whipstitch to B.

Whipstitch to A #2.

Whipstitch to F.

COLOR KEY
Eggs & Bunny Basket

EMBROIDERY FLOSS	DMC®
■ Black ½ yd. [0.5m]	#310

WORSTED-WEIGHT	NEED-LOFT®
□ White 30 yds. [27.4m]	#41
Yellow 25 yds. [22.9m]	#57
Bt. Blue 20 yds. [18.3m]	#60
Fern 20 yds. [18.3m]	#23

WORSTED-WEIGHT	NEED-LOFT®
Pink 20 yds. [18.3m]	#07
Tangerine 20 yds. [18.3m]	#11
Bt. Purple 10 yds. [9.1m]	#64
Eggshell 2 yds. [1.8m]	#39
Watermelon 1 yd. [0.9m]	#55

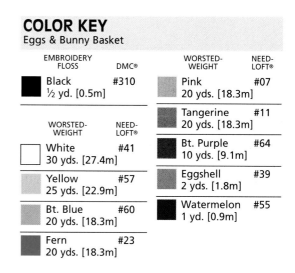

each Front A, lightly stuffing each Egg with fiberfill as you work.

5: With matching colors, whipstitch A and B pieces together and to F as indicated, forming Basket.

A – Egg #3 Front and Backing
(22w x 29h-hole pieces)
Cut 2; work 1 for Front & leave
1 unworked for Backing.

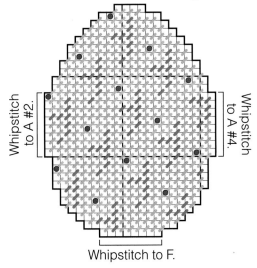

Whipstitch to A #2.

Whipstitch to A #4.

Whipstitch to F.

A – Egg #2 Front and Backing
(22w x 29h-hole pieces)
Cut 2; work 1 for Front & leave
1 unworked for Backing.

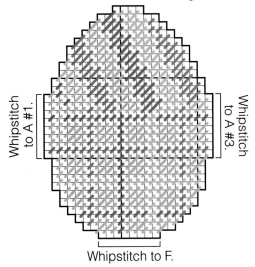

Whipstitch to A #1.

Whipstitch to A #3.

Whipstitch to F.

A – Egg #5 Front and Backing
(22w x 29h-hole pieces)
Cut 2; work 1 for Front & leave
1 unworked for Backing.

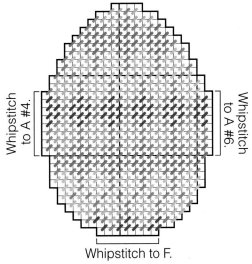

Whipstitch to A #4.

Whipstitch to A #6.

Whipstitch to F.

A – Egg #4 Front and Backing
(22w x 29h-hole pieces)
Cut 2; work 1 for Front & leave
1 unworked for Backing.

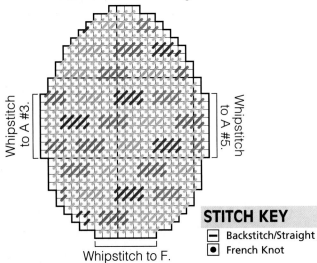

Whipstitch to A #3.

Whipstitch to A #5.

Whipstitch to F.

STITCH KEY
— Backstitch/Straight
• French Knot

COLOR KEY
Eggs & Bunny Basket

EMBROIDERY FLOSS	DMC®		WORSTED-WEIGHT	NEED-LOFT®
■ Black ½ yd. [0.5m]	#310		▨ Pink 20 yds. [18.3m]	#07
			▨ Tangerine 20 yds. [18.3m]	#11
WORSTED-WEIGHT	**NEED-LOFT®**		▨ Bt. Purple 10 yds. [9.1m]	#64
□ White 30 yds. [27.4m]	#41		▨ Eggshell 2 yds. [1.8m]	#39
▨ Yellow 25 yds. [22.9m]	#57		▨ Watermelon 1 yd. [0.9m]	#55
▨ Bt. Blue 20 yds. [18.3m]	#60			
▨ Fern 20 yds. [18.3m]	#23			

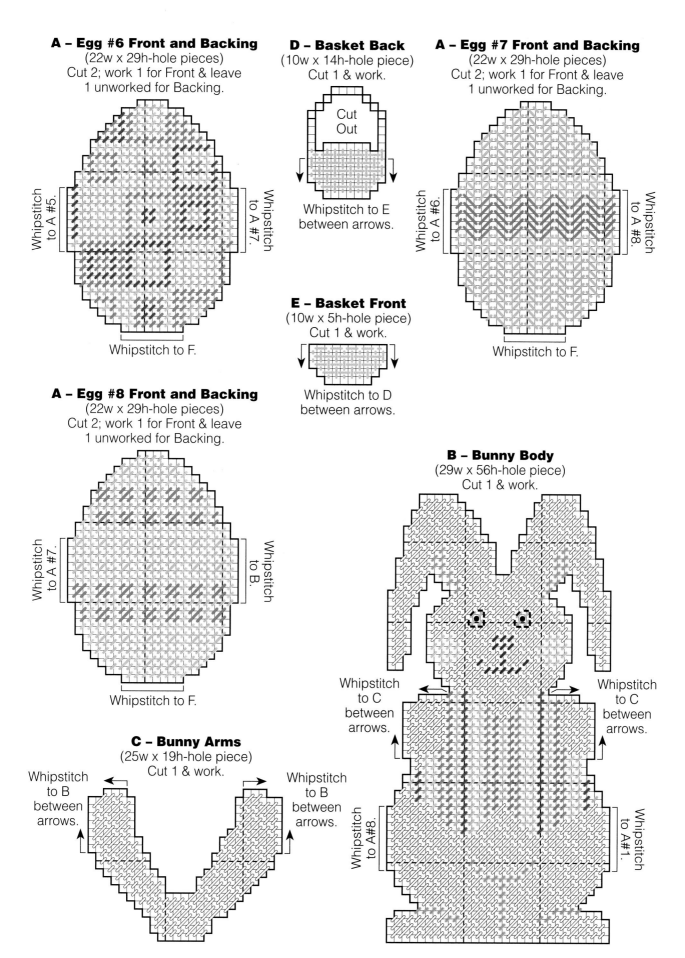

A – Egg #6 Front and Backing
(22w x 29h-hole pieces)
Cut 2; work 1 for Front & leave
1 unworked for Backing.

Whipstitch to A #5.

Whipstitch to A #7.

Whipstitch to F.

D – Basket Back
(10w x 14h-hole piece)
Cut 1 & work.

Cut
Out

Whipstitch to E
between arrows.

A – Egg #7 Front and Backing
(22w x 29h-hole pieces)
Cut 2; work 1 for Front & leave
1 unworked for Backing.

Whipstitch to A #6.

Whipstitch to A #8.

Whipstitch to F.

E – Basket Front
(10w x 5h-hole piece)
Cut 1 & work.

Whipstitch to D
between arrows.

A – Egg #8 Front and Backing
(22w x 29h-hole pieces)
Cut 2; work 1 for Front & leave
1 unworked for Backing.

Whipstitch to A #7.

Whipstitch to B.

Whipstitch to F.

B – Bunny Body
(29w x 56h-hole piece)
Cut 1 & work.

Whipstitch to C between arrows.

Whipstitch to C between arrows.

Whipstitch to A#8.

Whipstitch to A #1.

C – Bunny Arms
(25w x 19h-hole piece)
Cut 1 & work.

Whipstitch to B between arrows.

Whipstitch to B between arrows.

Holidays on Parade **33**

Easter Magnets

Designed by Victoria Bailey

Decorate your kitchen this Easter with these cute holiday fridgies.

SIZE: Each Magnet is about 2" x 2" [5.1cm x 5.1cm]

SKILL LEVEL: Average

MATERIALS:
- ½ sheet of 10-mesh plastic canvas
- Two 7mm and one 5mm wiggle eye
- ¾ yd. [0.7m] of pink ⅛" [3mm] satin ribbon
- Five ¾" [19mm] artificial flowers of choice
- One 5mm pink pom-pom
- Five ⅝" [16mm] round magnets
- Craft glue or glue gun
- No. 3 pearl cotton (coton perle) (for amounts see Color Key)

CUTTING INSTRUCTIONS:
A: For Large Rabbit, cut one according to graph.
B: For Small Rabbit, cut one according to graph.
C: For Egg #1, cut one according to graph.
D: For Egg #2, cut one according to graph.
E: For Basket, cut one according to graph.

STITCHING INSTRUCTIONS:
1: Using colors and stitches indicated, work pieces according to graphs; with matching colors as shown in photo, overcast edges of pieces.

2: Using colors and embroidery stitches indicated, embroider detail on C-E pieces as indicated on graphs.

NOTE: Cut ribbon into three 9" [22.9cm] lengths; tie one length into a bow.

3: Wrap one length around one ear of Large Rabbit and tie in a knot; glue one flower and 7mm wiggle eyes to right side of Large Rabbit as shown in photo. Wrap one length around neck of Small Rabbit and tie in a knot; glue one flower, pom-pom and 5mm wiggle eye to right side of Small Rabbit as shown. Glue bow and three flowers to right side of Basket as shown.

4: Glue one magnet to wrong side of each worked piece.

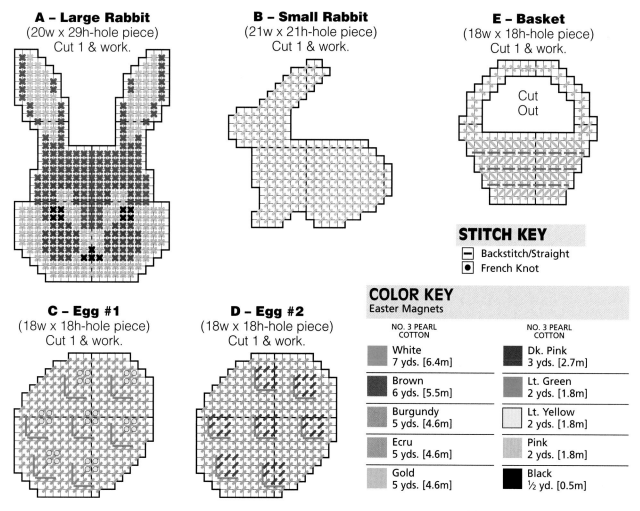

A – Large Rabbit
(20w x 29h-hole piece)
Cut 1 & work.

B – Small Rabbit
(21w x 21h-hole piece)
Cut 1 & work.

E – Basket
(18w x 18h-hole piece)
Cut 1 & work.

Cut Out

STITCH KEY
- Backstitch/Straight
- French Knot

C – Egg #1
(18w x 18h-hole piece)
Cut 1 & work.

D – Egg #2
(18w x 18h-hole piece)
Cut 1 & work.

COLOR KEY
Easter Magnets

NO. 3 PEARL COTTON		NO. 3 PEARL COTTON	
White	7 yds. [6.4m]	Dk. Pink	3 yds. [2.7m]
Brown	6 yds. [5.5m]	Lt. Green	2 yds. [1.8m]
Burgundy	5 yds. [4.6m]	Lt. Yellow	2 yds. [1.8m]
Ecru	5 yds. [4.6m]	Pink	2 yds. [1.8m]
Gold	5 yds. [4.6m]	Black	½ yd. [0.5m]

Easter Bunny

Designed by Lee Lindeman

Watch this adorable bunny bring smiles into your home this spring.

SIZE: 6" x 10" tall [15.2cm x 25.4cm]

Bunnie

SKILL LEVEL: Challenging

MATERIALS:
- One sheet of 7-mesh plastic canvas
- Three white 5/16" [8mm] buttons and two white 1/8" [3mm] flat sew-on buttons
- Two black 5mm half round bead eyes
- One black 15mm rabbit nose
- One white 3/4" [19mm] pom-pom
- 1/2 yd. [0.5m] multi-colored 1" [2.5cm] ribbon
- One 1/4" [6mm] and one 3/8" [10mm] dowel rod
- 10-yd. [9.1m] spool of rose 18-gauge wire
- One 5/8" x 7/8" [16mm x 22mm] miniature plastic Easter egg with hanger
- One straight pin
- White thread and sewing needle
- Polyester fiberfill
- Sandpaper or steel file
- 1/2 yd. [0.5m] length of heavy gold metallic cord
- Craft glue or glue gun
- Six-strand embroidery floss (for amount see Color Key)
- Worsted-weight or plastic canvas yarn (for amounts see Color Key)

CUTTING INSTRUCTIONS:
A: For Bunny Head Front and Back, cut one each according to graphs.
B: For Bunny Body Front and Back, cut one each according to graphs.
C: For Bunny Hands Front and Back, cut two each according to graphs.
D: For Bunny Feet Tops and Bottoms, cut two each according to graphs.

STITCHING INSTRUCTIONS:
1: Using colors indicated and continental stitch, work pieces according to graphs; with matching colors, overcast indicated edges of pieces.

2: Using six strands floss and backstitch, embroider detail on Front A and Back B as indicated on graphs.

NOTE: For neck, tightly coil wire around 3/8" dowel

NOTES:
around 1/4" a...
2½" [6.4cm] in ...
For each leg (make ...
dowel rod until leg is ....ng 3 [7.6cm] in
length; cut wire from spool.

4: Using two strands floss and sewing needle, sew 5/16" buttons to Front B and 1/8" buttons to Back B as indicated. With matching colors, whipstitch B pieces wrong sides together, stuffing Body generously with fiberfill and securing arms, legs and neck in place (see photo) before closing.

5: For each Hand (make 2), with white, whipstitch one C#1 and one C#2 wrong sides together, securing over end of one arm before closing.

NOTE: Cut cord in half; tie each length into a bow.

6: For each Foot (make 2), with white, whipstitch one D#1 and one D#2 wrong sides together, stuffing lightly with fiberfill and securing over end of one leg before closing. Glue one bow to each foot as shown.

7: For collar, using white thread and sewing needle, gather one long edge of ribbon around neck and tie thread into a knot at back to secure.

NOTE: Remove shank from back of nose; file smooth.

8: Glue eyes and nose to Front A as indicated; glue pom-pom to Back B as indicated. Using straight pin, attach Easter egg to one Hand as shown.

A – Bunny Head Front
(16w x 24h-hole piece)
Cut 1 & work.

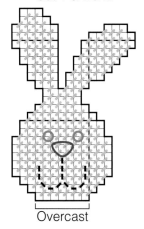

Overcast

B – Bunny Body Front
(18w x 21h-hole piece)
Cut 1 & work.

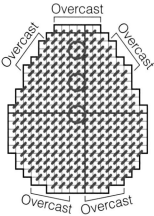

Overcast

B – Bunny Body Back
(18w x 21h-hole piece)
Cut 1 & work.

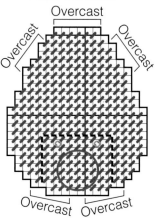

Overcast

A – Bunny Head Back
(16w x 24h-hole piece)
Cut 1 & work.

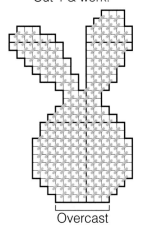

Overcast

D – Bunny Foot Top
(8w x 11h-hole pieces)
Cut 2 & work.

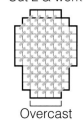

Overcast

D – Bunny Foot Bottom
(8w x 11h-hole pieces)
Cut 2 & work.

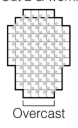

Overcast

PLACEMENT KEY
- ⊙ Eyes
- ☐ Nose
- ⊙ Pom-Pom

ATTACHMENT KEY
- ⊙ ⁵⁄₁₆" Button
- ⊙ ⅛" Button

STITCH KEY
- ▬ Backstitch

COLOR KEY
Easter Bunny

EMBROIDERY FLOSS	DMC®
■ Black 2 yds. [1.8m]	#310

WORSTED WEIGHT	
■ Rose 20 yds. [18.3m]	

WORSTED WEIGHT	NEED-LOFT®
■ White 20 yds. [18.3m]	#41
■ Pink 4 yds. [3.7m]	#07

C – Bunny Hand Front
(6w x 6h-hole pieces)
Cut 2 & work.

Overcast

C – Bunny Hand Back
(6w x 6h-hole pieces)
Cut 2 & work.

Overcast

Easter Chick

Designed by Lee Lindeman

He wiggles and jiggles but you won't hear a peep out of this Easter Chick!

SIZE: 5" x 5½" tall [12.7cm x 14cm], when sitting

SKILL LEVEL: Challenging

MATERIALS:
- One sheet of 7-mesh plastic canvas
- 1 yd. [0.9m] green ½" [13mm] voile ribbon
- One yellow ¾" [19mm] ribbon rose with leaves
- Scrap piece each of orange and red buckram or plastic foam sheet
- One ¼" [6mm] and one ⅜" [10mm] dowel rod
- 10-yd. [9.1m] spool of lemon 18-gauge wire
- Polyester fiberfill
- Craft glue or glue gun
- Six-strand embroidery floss (for amount see Color Key)
- Worsted-weight or plastic canvas yarn (for amounts see Color Key)

CUTTING INSTRUCTIONS:
A: For Chick Head Front and Back, cut one each according to graphs.
B: For Chick Body Front and Back, cut two (one for Front and one for Back) according to graph.
C: For Chick Wings #1 and #2, cut two each according to graphs.
D: For Chick Feet, cut four according to graph.
E: For Chick Tail, cut two according to graph.

STITCHING INSTRUCTIONS:
1: Using colors indicated and continental stitch, work pieces according to graphs; with matching colors, overcast indicated edges of A-D pieces.

2: Using six strands floss and French knot, embroider eyes on Front A as indicated on graph.

NOTE: For neck, tightly coil wire around ⅜" dowel rod until neck is approximately ¾" [19mm] in length; cut wire from spool.

3: For Head, with yellow, whipstitch A pieces wrong sides together, stuffing face lightly with fiberfill and securing neck in place (see photo) before closing.

*NOTES: For each arm (make 2), tightly coil wire around ¼" dowel rod until arm is approximately 1" [2.5cm] in length; cut wire from spool.
For each leg (make 2), tightly coil wire around ¼" dowel rod until leg is approximately 2½" [6.4cm] in length; cut wire from spool.*

4: With yellow, whipstitch B pieces wrong sides together, stuffing Body generously with fiberfill and securing arms and neck in place (see photo) before closing. Twist legs into place as indicated on B graph.

5: For each Wing (make 2), with yellow, whipstitch one C#1 and one C#2 wrong sides together, securing over end of one arm before closing.

6: For each Foot (make 2), with tangerine, whipstitch two D pieces wrong sides together, securing over end of one leg before closing.

7: For sash, drape ribbon around Chick and tie into a bow (see photo); glue rose to sash and sash to Chick as shown.

8: Cut beak and comb from buckram or foam sheets according to Beak and Comb Patterns; glue to Chick's Head (see photo). For Tail, with yellow, whipstitch E pieces wrong sides together; glue to Body Back as indicated.

A – Chick Head Front
(10w x 11h-hole piece)
Cut 1 & work.

Overcast

A – Chick Head Back
(10w x 11h-hole piece)
Cut 1 & work.

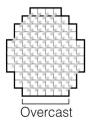

Overcast

E – Chick Tail
(10w x 7h-hole pieces)
Cut 2 & work.

Glue

D – Chick Foot
(9w x 10h-hole pieces)
Cut 4 & work.

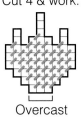

Overcast

C – Chick Wing #1
(9w x 11h-hole pieces)
Cut 2 & work.

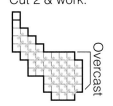

Overcast

C – Chick Wing #2
(9w x 11h-hole pieces)
Cut 2 & work.

Overcast

B – Chick Body Front and Back
(20w x 19h-hole pieces)
Cut 2. Work 1 for Front & 1 for Back.

Overcast

Overcast

Overcast

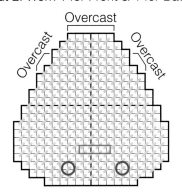

Comb Pattern
(actual size)

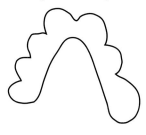

Beak Patterns
(actual sizes)

Upper Beak

Lower Beak

Fold Line

STITCH KEY
⊙ French Knot

PLACEMENT KEY
☐ Beak
☐ Legs
☐ Tail

COLOR KEY
Easter Chick

EMBROIDERY FLOSS

■ Black
¼ yd. [0.2m]

	WORSTED WEIGHT	NEED-LOFT®
Yellow 30 yds. [27.4m]		#57
Tangerine 4 yds. [3.7m]		#11
Watermelon ½ yd. [0.5m]		#55

Cross Magnet

Designed by Mary Perry

Remember the reason for the season with this inspirational magnet.

Cross Magnet
(26w x 38h-hole piece)
Cut 1 & work.

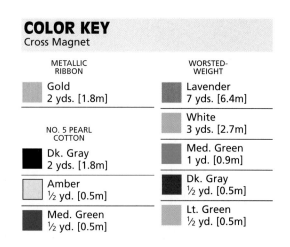

SIZE: 4" x 5¾" [10.2cm x 14.6cm]

SKILL LEVEL: Easy

MATERIALS:
- ½ sheet of 7-mesh plastic canvas
- 2" [5.1cm] piece of ½" [13mm] magnetic strip
- 1/16" [2mm] metallic ribbon (for amount see Color Key)
- No. 5 pearl cotton (coton perle) (for amounts see Color Key)
- Worsted-weight or plastic canvas yarn (for amounts see Color Key)

CUTTING INSTRUCTIONS:
For Cross Magnet, cut one according to graph.

STITCHING INSTRUCTIONS:
1: Using colors indicated and continental stitch, work Cross Magnet according to graph; with matching colors as shown in photo, overcast edges.

2: Using pearl cotton and embroidery stitches indicated, embroider detail as indicated on graph.

3: Glue magnetic strip to wrong side of Magnet.

STITCH KEY
- ⊟ Backstitch/Straight
- ⊡ French Knot

COLOR KEY
Cross Magnet

METALLIC RIBBON		WORSTED-WEIGHT	
Gold 2 yds. [1.8m]		Lavender 7 yds. [6.4m]	
NO. 5 PEARL COTTON		White 3 yds. [2.7m]	
Dk. Gray 2 yds. [1.8m]		Med. Green 1 yd. [0.9m]	
Amber ½ yd. [0.5m]		Dk. Gray ½ yd. [0.5m]	
Med. Green ½ yd. [0.5m]		Lt. Green ½ yd. [0.5m]	

Happy Mother's Day!

Show your mother just how special she is by creating a personalized gift just for her.

Mother's Day Roses

Designed by Sheri Lautenschlager

Give your mom an everlasting rose on her special day.

SIZES: Bowl is 11½" across x 3¾" tall [29.2cm x 9.5cm]; Candle Holder is 6½" across x 2½" tall [16.5cm x 6.4cm]; Wind Chimes are 6½" across x 2½" [16.5cm x 6.4cm], not including chimes and hanger; Crystal Hanger is 5" across x 1½" tall [12.7cm x 3.8cm], not including hanger; Hook is 4½" x 2" x 7¾" [11.4cm x 5.1cm x 19.7cm]; Plant Poke is 2¾" x 2¾" [7cm x 7cm], not including stick. Excluding Plant poke, measurements do not include Butterflies

SKILL LEVEL: Challenging

MATERIALS:
- Ten sheets of 7-mesh plastic canvas
- ¼ sheet of 10-mesh plastic canvas
- Five silver ¼" x about 3" [0.6cm x 7.6cm] aluminum chimes with pre-drilled holes at one end
- 1 yd. [0.9m] of 4mm x 7mm silver chain
- One silver 7mm jump ring
- Twelve silver 10mm jump rings
- One ¾" [19mm] bone ring
- Silver paint
- Six ⅛"-wide x ¾"-long [3mm x 19mm] wire springs
- Eight 3mm wiggle eyes
- Two 4mm movable eyes
- Two crystal 31mm x 31mm acrylic hearts
- Four amethyst 7mm x 15mm navette shaped acrylic rhinestones
- Four turquoise 7mm x 15mm navette shaped acrylic rhinestones
- Four lavender 13mm x 8mm pear shaped acrylic rhinestones
- Six light blue 13mm x 8mm pear shaped acrylic rhinestones
- Four amethyst 18mm x 8mm pear shaped acrylic rhinestones;
- Four pink 18mm x 8mm pear shaped / acrylic rhinestones
- Four amethyst 5mm round acrylic rhinestones
- Two lavender 5mm round acrylic rhinestones
- Two turquoise 5mm round acrylic rhinestones
- Two pink 5mm round acrylic rhinestones
- Two light blue 5mm round acrylic rhinestones
- 12½ yds. [11.4m] of 20-gauge silver wire
- 14" [35.6cm] of 16-gauge green stem wire
- 18" [45.7cm] of 18-gauge silver wire
- 1 yd. [0.9m] of 26-gauge black wire
- One 12" [30.5cm] floral stake
- Craft glue or glue gun
- Six-strand embroidery floss (for amount see Color Key
- Worsted-weight or plastic canvas yarn (for amounts see Color Key)

CUTTING INSTRUCTIONS:
NOTE: Cut V pieces from 10-mesh and remaining pieces from 7-mesh canvas.

A: For Large Rose Inner Petals, cut five according to graph.
B: For Large Rose Inner Petal Base, cut one according to graph.
C: For Large Rose Outer Petals, cut five according to graph.
D: For Large Rose Outer Petal Base, cut one according to graph.
E: For Large Rose Leaves, cut four according to graph.
F: For Large Rose Leaf Base, cut two according to graph.
G: For Medium Rose Outer Petals, cut ten according to graph.
H: For Medium Rose Outer Petal Bases, cut two according to graph.
I: For Medium Rose Center Petals, cut ten according to graph.
J: For Medium Rose Center Petal Bases, cut two according to graph.
K: For Medium Rose Inner Petals, cut three according to graph.
L: For Medium Rose Inner Petal Base, cut one according to graph.
M: For Medium Rose Calyxes, cut two according to graph.
N: For Small Rose Outer Petals, cut ten according to graph.
O: For Small Rose Outer Petal Bases, cut two

according to graph.

P: For Small Rose Center Petals, cut ten according to graph.

Q: For Small Rose Center Petal Bases, cut two according to graph.

R: For Small Rose Inner Petals, cut six according to graph.

S: For Small Rose Inner Petal Bases, cut two according to graph.

T: For Small Rose Calyx, cut one according to graph.

U: For Small Rose Stems, cut two according to graph.

V: For Small and Large Ladybugs, cut five (four for Small Ladybug and one for Large Ladybug) according to graphs.

W: For Large Butterfly Wings #1 and #2, cut one each according to graphs.

X: For Medium Butterfly Wings #1 and #2, cut one each according to graphs.

Y: For Small Light Blue, Turquoise, Medium Purple, and Magenta Butterfly Wings #1 and #2, cut one each according to graphs.

STITCHING INSTRUCTIONS:

NOTE: Separate 4-ply yarn into 2-ply for stitching and overcasting on 10-mesh canvas.

1: Using colors and stitches indicated, work pieces according to graphs.

NOTE: Cut 20-gauge wire into six 2½" [6.4cm], ten 3½" [8.9cm], thirteen 4" [10.2cm], ten 4½" [11.4cm], ten 5" [12.7cm], four 7" [17.8cm], thirteen 8½" [21.6cm], five 9" [22.9cm], and four 13" [33cm] lengths.

2: Holding one corresponding wire length to indicated edges of each Petal, Leaf and Calyx, omitting attachment edges, with black for Ladybug head areas and with indicated and matching colors, overcast edges of A, C, E, G, I, K, M, N, P, R, T, and V-Y pieces. Omitting attachment edges, with medium green, whipstitch edges of F pieces together.

3: Using six strands floss and black yarn (Separate into individual plies, if desired.) and embroidery stitches indicated, embroider detail on V-Y pieces as indicated on graphs.

4: For Small Roses (make 2), whipstitch and assemble corresponding Small Rose Petals and

Petal Bases according to Rose Assembly Diagram on page 48.

NOTE: Cut one 1" [2.5cm] and one 8" [30.5cm] length of 18-gauge wire.

5: For Crystal Hanger Rose, glue one Small Rose to center right side of Small Rose Calyx. Bend up leaves of Calyx; shape and glue to Rose petals as shown. Bend 1" wire into a triangle and attach to one acrylic heart as shown in photo. Insert one end of 8" wire into Small Rose Calyx and bend remaining end into a loop over Small Rose as shown; attach acrylic heart to wire as shown.

6: For Rose Hook, holding 16-gauge wire between pieces as indicated, with medium green, whipstitch U pieces together, forming Stem. Glue remaining Small Rose to Stem and bend bottom of Stem into a hook shape (see photo).

7: For Medium Roses (make 2), whipstitch and assemble corresponding Medium Rose Petals and Petal Bases according to Rose Assembly Diagram (NOTE: Omit Inner Petal on one Medium Rose assembly.). Glue one Medium Rose to center right side of each Medium Rose Calyx. Bend up leaves of Calyx; shape and glue to Rose petals as shown.

NOTES: Cut chain into one 3½" [8.9cm], one 3¾" [9.5cm], two 4" [10.2cm], one 4¼" [10.8cm], one 4½" [11.4cm], and one 5" [12.7cm] length.
Cut one 1" [2.5cm] and one 2¼" [5.7cm] length of 18-gauge wire.
Paint bone ring; let dry.

8: Assemble Medium Rose (with Inner Petal assembly), chains, bone ring, jump rings, wire, one acrylic heart and chimes according to Wind Chimes Assembly Diagram on page 50. Insert candle and glass cup in center of remaining Medium Rose, forming Candle Holder.

9: For Bowl, omitting Inner Petal assembly, whipstitch and assemble corresponding Large Rose Petals and Petal Bases according to Rose Assembly Diagram. With medium green, whipstitch E and F pieces together as indicated, forming Large Rose Calyx; overcast unfinished edges. Glue Large Rose to center right side of Large Rose Calyx. Bend up leaves of Calyx; shape and glue to Rose petals as shown.

10: For each Butterfly, with black, whipstitch corresponding Wing Pieces together as indicated. Matching stone color to color of Butterfly, glue one navette or pear stone to each wing segment and one round stone to each tail segment on Butterfly as shown in photo.

NOTE: Cut 26-gauge black wire into one 5" [12.7cm], five 4" [10.2cm], one 1½" [3.8cm], and four 1" [2.5cm] lengths.

11: Fold each wire length in half, then curl each wire end, forming Antennae. Glue 5" antennae to Large Butterfly, one 4" antennae to each

remaining Butterfly, 1½" antennae to Large Ladybug and one 1" antennae to each Small Ladybug as shown in photo. Glue or thread one wire spring to center wrong side of each Butterfly. Glue large eyes to Large Ladybug and two small eyes to each Small Ladybug.

12: Glue or thread wire spring on Large Butterfly to one petal and Large Ladybug to one leaf on Rose Bowl as shown. Glue one Small Butterfly and one Small Ladybug to each remaining Rose as shown. For Plant Poke, glue wire spring on Medium Butterfly to one end of floral stake.

B – Large Rose Inner Petal Base
(33w x 33h-hole piece)
Cut 1 from 7-mesh & work.

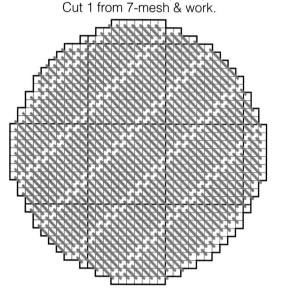

A – Large Rose Inner Petal
(27w x 27h-hole pieces)
Cut 5 from 7-mesh & work.

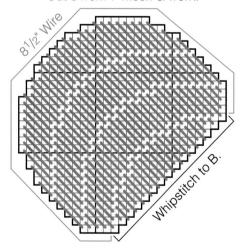

8½" Wire

Whipstitch to B.

C – Large Rose Outer Petal
(28w x 28h-hole pieces)
Cut 5 from 7-mesh & work.

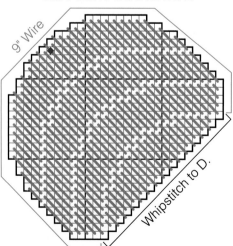

9" Wire

Whipstitch to D.

D – Large Rose Outer Petal Base
(35w x 35h-hole piece)
Cut 1 from 7-mesh & work.

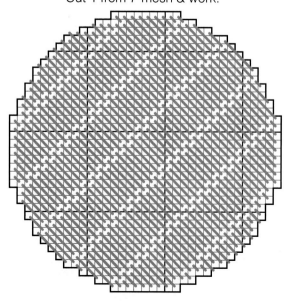

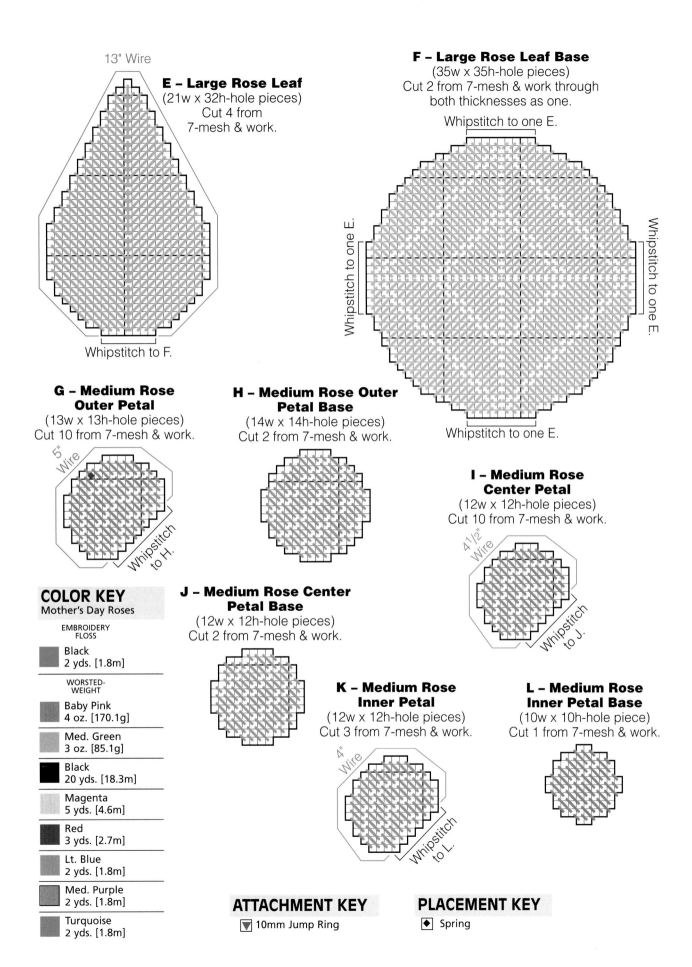

13" Wire

E – Large Rose Leaf
(21w x 32h-hole pieces)
Cut 4 from
7-mesh & work.

Whipstitch to F.

F – Large Rose Leaf Base
(35w x 35h-hole pieces)
Cut 2 from 7-mesh & work through
both thicknesses as one.

Whipstitch to one E.

Whipstitch to one E.

Whipstitch to one E.

Whipstitch to one E.

**G – Medium Rose
Outer Petal**
(13w x 13h-hole pieces)
Cut 10 from 7-mesh & work.

5" Wire

Whipstitch to H.

**H – Medium Rose Outer
Petal Base**
(14w x 14h-hole pieces)
Cut 2 from 7-mesh & work.

**I – Medium Rose
Center Petal**
(12w x 12h-hole pieces)
Cut 10 from 7-mesh & work.

4½" Wire

Whipstitch to J.

COLOR KEY
Mother's Day Roses

EMBROIDERY
FLOSS

Black
2 yds. [1.8m]

WORSTED-
WEIGHT

Baby Pink
4 oz. [170.1g]

Med. Green
3 oz. [85.1g]

Black
20 yds. [18.3m]

Magenta
5 yds. [4.6m]

Red
3 yds. [2.7m]

Lt. Blue
2 yds. [1.8m]

Med. Purple
2 yds. [1.8m]

Turquoise
2 yds. [1.8m]

**J – Medium Rose Center
Petal Base**
(12w x 12h-hole pieces)
Cut 2 from 7-mesh & work.

**K – Medium Rose
Inner Petal**
(12w x 12h-hole pieces)
Cut 3 from 7-mesh & work.

4" Wire

Whipstitch to L.

**L – Medium Rose
Inner Petal Base**
(10w x 10h-hole piece)
Cut 1 from 7-mesh & work.

ATTACHMENT KEY
▼ 10mm Jump Ring

PLACEMENT KEY
◆ Spring

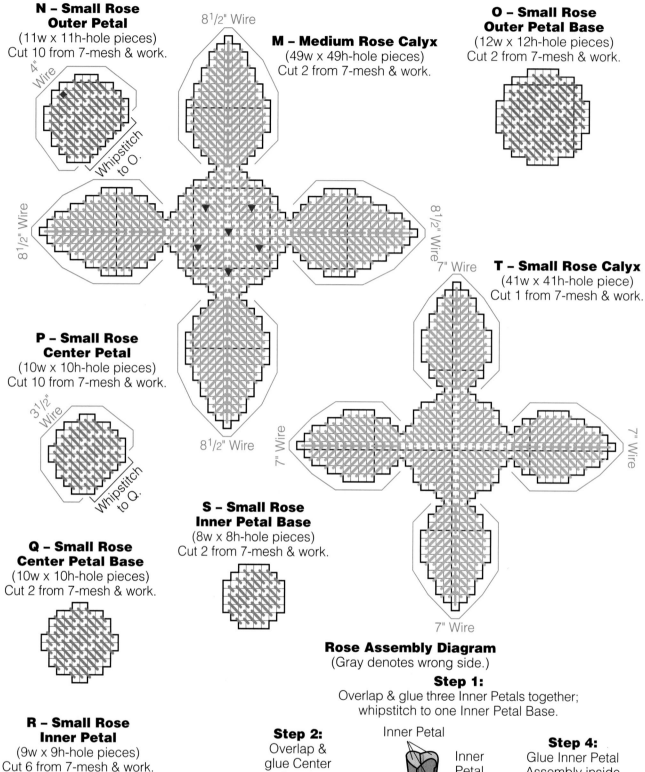

N – Small Rose Outer Petal
(11w x 11h-hole pieces)
Cut 10 from 7-mesh & work.

4" Wire

Whipstitch to O.

8 1/2" Wire

M – Medium Rose Calyx
(49w x 49h-hole pieces)
Cut 2 from 7-mesh & work.

O – Small Rose Outer Petal Base
(12w x 12h-hole pieces)
Cut 2 from 7-mesh & work.

8 1/2" Wire

8 1/2" Wire

P – Small Rose Center Petal
(10w x 10h-hole pieces)
Cut 10 from 7-mesh & work.

3 1/2" Wire

Whipstitch to Q.

8 1/2" Wire

7" Wire

T – Small Rose Calyx
(41w x 41h-hole piece)
Cut 1 from 7-mesh & work.

7" Wire

7" Wire

7" Wire

S – Small Rose Inner Petal Base
(8w x 8h-hole pieces)
Cut 2 from 7-mesh & work.

Q – Small Rose Center Petal Base
(10w x 10h-hole pieces)
Cut 2 from 7-mesh & work.

Rose Assembly Diagram
(Gray denotes wrong side.)

Step 1:
Overlap & glue three Inner Petals together;
whipstitch to one Inner Petal Base.

Step 2:
Overlap & glue Center Petals together; whipstitch to one Center Petal Base.

Inner Petal

Inner Petal Base

Center Petal

Center Petal Base

Step 4:
Glue Inner Petal Assembly inside Center Petal Assembly & Center Petal Assembly inside Outer Petal Assembly; bend wires on petals to shape as desired.

R – Small Rose Inner Petal
(9w x 9h-hole pieces)
Cut 6 from 7-mesh & work.

2 1/2" Wire

Whipstitch to S.

Step 3:
(Not Shown)
Overlap & glue Outer Petals together;
whipstitch to one Outer Petal Base.

Y – Small Light Blue Butterfly Wing #1
(6w x 13h-hole piece)
Cut 1 from 7-mesh & work.

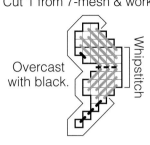

Overcast with black.

Whipstitch

Y – Small Light Blue Butterfly Wing #2
(6w x 13h-hole piece)
Cut 1 from 7-mesh & work.

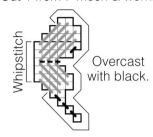

Whipstitch

Overcast with black.

Y – Small Magenta Butterfly Wing #1
(6w x 13h-hole piece)
Cut 1 from 7-mesh & work.

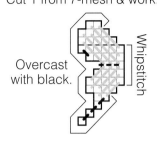

Overcast with black.

Whipstitch

Y – Small Magenta Butterfly Wing #2
(6w x 13h-hole piece)
Cut 1 from 7-mesh & work.

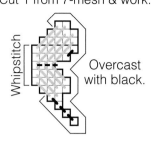

Whipstitch

Overcast with black.

Y – Small Turquoise Butterfly Wing #1
(6w x 13h-hole piece)
Cut 1 from 7-mesh & work.

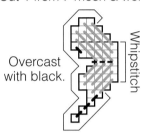

Overcast with black.

Whipstitch

Y – Small Turquoise Butterfly Wing #2
(6w x 13h-hole piece)
Cut 1 from 7-mesh & work.

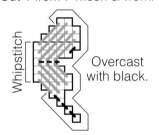

Whipstitch

Overcast with black.

Y – Small Purple Butterfly Wing #1
(6w x 13h-hole piece)
Cut 1 from 7-mesh & work.

Overcast with black.

Whipstitch

Y – Small Purple Butterfly Wing #2
(6w x 13h-hole piece)
Cut 1 from 7-mesh & work.

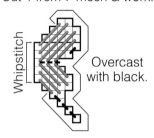

Whipstitch

Overcast with black.

ATTACHMENT KEY

▼ 10mm Jump Ring

X – Medium Butterfly Wing #1
(8w x 16h-hole piece)
Cut 1 from 7-mesh & work.

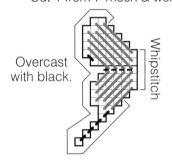

Overcast with black.

Whipstitch

X – Medium Butterfly Wing #2
(8w x 16h-hole piece)
Cut 1 from 7-mesh & work.

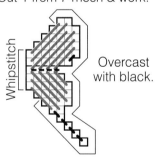

Whipstitch

Overcast with black.

COLOR KEY
Mother's Day Roses

EMBROIDERY FLOSS

| | Black | 2 yds. [1.8m] |

WORSTED-WEIGHT

	Baby Pink	6 oz. [170.1g]
	Med. Green	3 oz. [85.1g]
	Black	20 yds. [18.3m]
	Magenta	5 yds. [4.6m]
	Red	3 yds. [2.7m]
	Lt. Blue	2 yds. [1.8m]
	Med. Purple	2 yds. [1.8m]
	Turquoise	2 yds. [1.8m]

STITCH KEY

− Backstitch/Straight
● French Knot

PLACEMENT KEY

◆ Spring

W – Large Butterfly Wing #1
(9w x 19h-hole piece)
Cut 1 from 7-mesh & work.

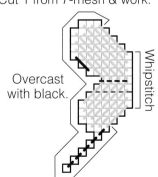

Overcast with black.

Whipstitch

W – Large Butterfly Wing #2
(9w x 19h-hole piece)
Cut 1 from 7-mesh & work.

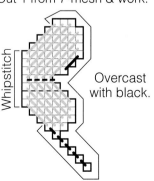

Whipstitch

Overcast with black.

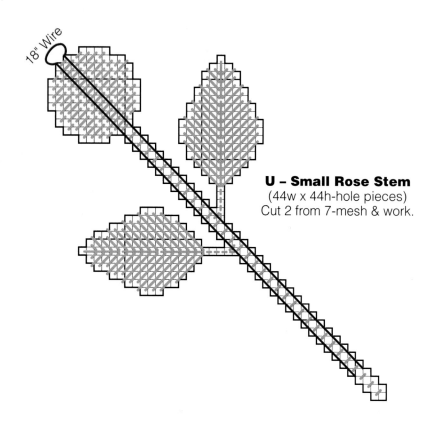

V – Small Ladybug
(5w x 5h-hole pieces)
Cut 4 from 10-mesh & work.

U – Small Rose Stem
(44w x 44h-hole pieces)
Cut 2 from 7-mesh & work.

V – Large Ladybug
(7w x 7h-hole piece)
Cut 1 from 10-mesh & work.

ATTACHMENT KEY
▼ 10mm Jump Ring

PLACEMENT KEY
◆ Spring

COLOR KEY
Mother's Day Roses

EMBROIDERY FLOSS

	Black
	2 yds. [1.8m]

WORSTED-WEIGHT

	Baby Pink
	6 oz. [170.1g]
	Med. Green
	3 oz. [85.1g]
	Black
	20 yds. [18.3m]
	Magenta
	5 yds. [4.6m]
	Red
	3 yds. [2.7m]
	Lt. Blue
	2 yds. [1.8m]
	Med. Purple
	2 yds. [1.8m]
	Turquoise
	2 yds. [1.8m]

STITCH KEY
— Backstitch/Straight
● French Knot

Wind Chime Assembly Diagram
(Leaves not shown & Rose shown in outline form for clarity.)

Step 1:
Insert 2¼" wire through center of Rose & Calyx; make a loop in each end of wire; attach one 4" chain, one 10mm jump ring & bone ring to top loop of wire for hanger.

Step 2:
Attach one 10mm jump ring to each ▼ hole & one to loop of wire on right side of Calyx; attach one end of one chain to each ring; attach 7mm jump ring to center chain & one 10mm jump ring to opposite end of each remaining chain.

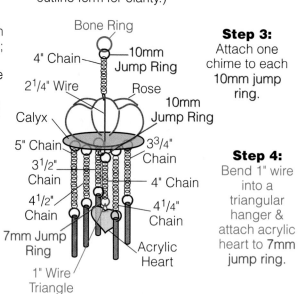

Bone Ring
10mm Jump Ring
4" Chain
2¼" Wire
Rose
Calyx
10mm Jump Ring
5" Chain
3¾" Chain
3½" Chain
4" Chain
4½" Chain
4¼" Chain
7mm Jump Ring
Acrylic Heart
1" Wire Triangle

Step 3:
Attach one chime to each 10mm jump ring.

Step 4:
Bend 1" wire into a triangular hanger & attach acrylic heart to 7mm jump ring.

Mother's Hanger Cover

Designed by Terry Ricioli

Mom will appreciate the pampering touch of handmade hanger covers.

SIZE: Hanger Cover is 5¼" x 17½" [13.3cm x 44.5cm]

SKILL LEVEL: Average

MATERIALS:
- Two sheets of 7-mesh plastic canvas
- One adult-size wire hanger
- 1 yd. [0.9m] pink ¼" [6mm] satin ribbon
- Craft glue or glue gun
- Worsted-weight or plastic canvas yarn (for amounts see Color Key)

CUTTING INSTRUCTIONS:
A: For Front Piece #1 and #2, cut one each according to graphs.
B: For Back Piece #1 and #2, cut one each according to graphs.

STITCHING INSTRUCTIONS:
1: Using colors and stitches indicated, work pieces according to graphs; omitting attachment areas, with pink, overcast edges.

NOTE: Cut one 12" [30.5cm] length of ribbon.

2: Wrap remaining ribbon around top of hanger as shown in photo, gluing as you wrap to secure. Tie 12" length into a bow around hanger as shown.

3: Holding hanger between, with pink, whipstitch Front and Back pieces wrong sides together as indicated on graphs.

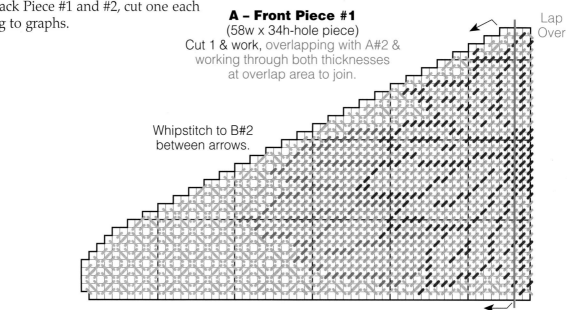

A – Front Piece #1
(58w x 34h-hole piece)
Cut 1 & work, overlapping with A#2 & working through both thicknesses at overlap area to join.

Lap Over

Whipstitch to B#2 between arrows.

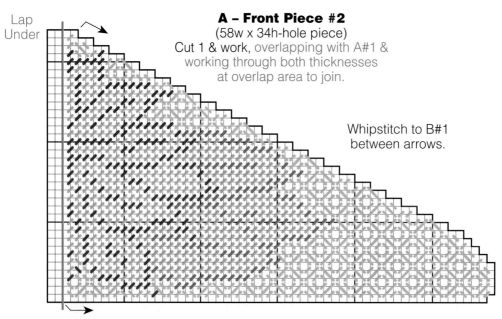

Lap Under

A – Front Piece #2
(58w x 34h-hole piece)
Cut 1 & work, overlapping with A#1 & working through both thicknesses at overlap area to join.

Whipstitch to B#1 between arrows.

B – Back Piece #1
(58w x 34h-hole piece)
Cut 1 & work, overlapping with B#2 &
working through both thicknesses
at overlap area to join.

Lap
Over

Whipstitch to A#2
between arrows.

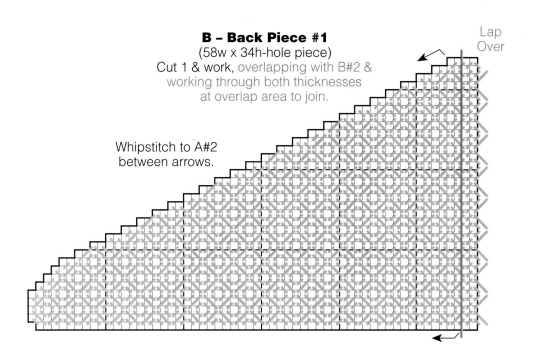

COLOR KEY
Mother's Hanger Cover

	WORSTED-WEIGHT	NEED-LOFT®
 Pink 75 yds. [68.6m]		#07
Lavender 12 yds. [11m]		#05
Burgundy 10 yds. [9.1m]		#03
Mermaid 8 yds. [7.3m]		#53
Forest 5 yds. [4.6m]		#29

B – Back Piece #2
(58w x 34h-hole piece)
Cut 1 & work, overlapping with B#1 &
working through both thicknesses
at overlap area to join.

Lap
Under

Whipstitch to A#1
between arrows.

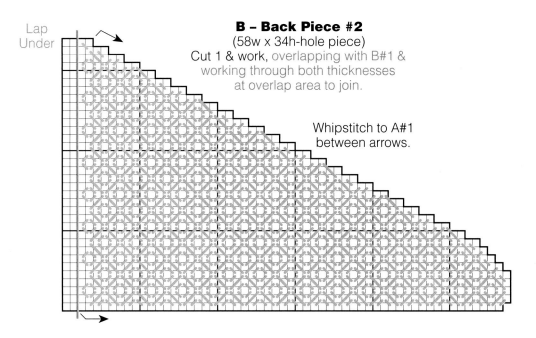

Secretary's Day!

Start the day off right by taking your secretary a cup of coffee and presenting her with a special hand-stitched gift.

Secretary's Memo Cube Holder

Designed by Judy Collishaw

Let your favorite secretary know you're thinking of her on her special day.

SIZE: About 4" x 4¼" x 5⅝" tall [10.2cm x 10.8cm x 14.3cm], and holds 3¼"-square [8.3cm] memos

SKILL LEVEL: Challenging

MATERIALS:
- One sheet of 7-mesh plastic canvas
- 4" [10.2cm] length of white fused 3mm pearl beads
- 5" [12.7cm] length of gold #28 beading wire
- 6" [15.2cm] length of black 16-gauge plastic coated wire
- Lemon curly doll hair
- Two round yellow toothpicks
- Black marker
- Pencil
- Size G crochet hook
- Craft glue or glue gun
- No. 5 pearl cotton (coton perlé) or six-strand embroidery floss (for amounts see Color Key)
- Worsted-weight or plastic canvas yarn (for amounts see Color Key)

CUTTING INSTRUCTIONS:
A: For Body Front, cut one according to graph.
B: For Body Back, cut one according to graph.
C: For Sides, cut two 23w x 19h-holes.
D: For Front Pieces, cut two 6w x 19h-holes.
E: For Bottom, cut one 23w x 23h-holes (no graph).
F: For Hand, cut one according to graph.
G: For Telephone, cut one according to graph.
H: For Steno Pad, cut one 6w x 11h-holes.

STITCHING INSTRUCTIONS:
NOTE: E is not worked.

1: Using colors and stitches indicated, work A-D and F-H pieces according to graphs. With rose, overcast indicated edge of A; with matching colors, overcast edges of F and G pieces.

2: Using pearl cotton or six strands floss and yarn (Separate yarn into individual plies, if desired.) in colors and embroidery stitches indicated, embroider detail on A-D and F and H pieces as indicated on graphs.

3: With matching colors as shown in photo, whipstitch A-E pieces together as indicated and according to Secretary's Memo Cube Holder Assembly Illustration on page 56; overcast unfinished edges.

NOTES: Wrap black wire around pencil to coil. Slide coils off pencil. Wrap gold wire around crochet hook to coil. Slide coils off hook.

4: Insert one end of black wire from front to back through u hole on G; glue to secure. Thread gold wire through holes at one short edge of H as shown in photo.

NOTE: For pencils (make 2), using marker, color one end of each toothpick.

5: Glue doll hair and pencils to Secretary's head as shown. Wrap beads around neck; glue to secure. Glue Hand, Telephone and Steno Pad to Front Pieces as shown.

A – Body Front
(23w x 25h-hole piece)
Cut 1 & work.

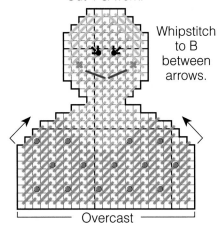

Whipstitch to B between arrows.

Overcast

B – Body Back
(23w x 36h-hole piece)
Cut 1 & work.

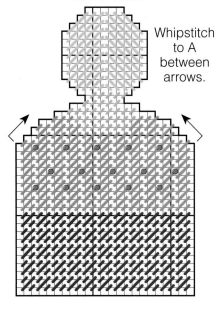

Whipstitch to A between arrows.

C – Side
(23w x 19h-hole pieces)
Cut 2 & work.

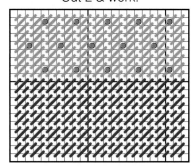

D – Front Piece
(6w x 19h-hole pieces)
Cut 2 & work.

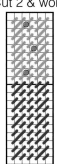

F – Hand
(7w x 6h-hole piece)
Cut 1 & work.

H – Steno Pad
(6w x 11h-hole piece)
Cut 1 & work.

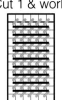

G – Telephone
(7w x 11h-hole piece)
Cut 1 & work.

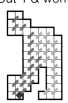

ATTACHMENT KEY
◈ Cord/Phone

STITCH KEY
− Backstitch/Straight
● French Knot

Secretary's Memo Cube Holder
Assembly Illustration
(Pieces are shown in different colors for contrast; gray denotes wrong side.)

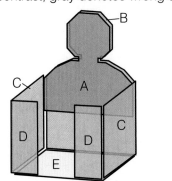

COLOR KEY
Secretary's Memo Cube Holder

NO. 3 PEARL COTTON OR FLOSS		DMC®
■	Black 2 yds. [1.8m]	#310
■	Red ½ yd. [0.5m]	#321

WORSTED-WEIGHT	
■	Burgundy 22 yds. [20.1m]
■	Rose 20 yds. [18.3m]
■	Peach 6 yds. [5.5m]
■	Baby Pink 4 yds. [3.7m]
■	Pale Yellow 2 yds. [1.8m]
■	Black 1 yd. [0.9m]
■	White 1 yd. [0.9m]
■	Red ½ yd. [0.5m]

Wedding Day!

Make a special day even more
memorable by stitching a bride and groom
cake topper made with love.

Cake Topper

Designed by Mary T. Cosgrove

Create this traditional cake topper as a keepsake for the happy couple.

SIZE: 6½" x 6¾" [16.5cm x 17.1cm], not including skewers.

SKILL LEVEL: Easy

MATERIALS:
- ½ sheet of 7-mesh plastic canvas
- Two gold ½" [13mm] liberty bells
- ½ sheet of metallic gold perforated paper
- Two 10" [25.4cm] wooden bamboo skewers
- Craft glue or glue gun
- Metallic craft cord (for amount see Color Key)
- Worsted-weight or plastic canvas yarn
  (for amounts see Color Key)

CUTTING INSTRUCTIONS:
A: For Bride and Groom, cut one according to graph.
B: For Heart, cut one according to graph.

STITCHING INSTRUCTIONS:
1: Using colors indicated and continental stitch, work pieces according to graphs. With matching colors as shown in photo, overcast edges of pieces.

2: Using cord and yarn in colors and embroidery stitches indicated, embroider detail on A as indicated on graph.

3: With Christmas red, tack bells to B as indicated. Glue wrong side of Bride and Groom to right side of Heart as shown in photo, forming Cake Topper.

NOTE: Using Cake Topper as a pattern, cut one backing from perforated paper ⅛" [3mm] smaller at all edges; glue backing to wrong side of Cake Topper.

4: Glue skewers to wrong side of Cake Topper (see photo).

COLOR KEY
Cake Topper

	CRAFT CORD	NEED-LOFT®
Gold 4 yds. [3.7m]		#01

	WORSTED-WEIGHT	NEED-LOFT®
Christmas Red 10 yds. [9.1m]		#02
White 6 yds. [5.5m]		#41
Black 4 yds. [3.7m]		#00
Gray 3 yds. [2.7m]		#38
Pink 2 yds. [1.8m]		#07

PLACEMENT KEY
◆ Bell

STITCH KEY
□ Backstitch/Straight

A – Bride and Groom
(29w x 34h-hole piece)
Cut 1 & work.

B – Heart
(44w x 32h-hole piece) Cut 1 & work.

Happy Father's Day!

*Show your love and appreciation to Dad
by giving him a dresser set
made expecially for him.*

Dad's Stuff

Designed by Dorothy Roller

Surprise Dad with a vanity set for keeping his personal belongings organized.

SIZES:
Tissue Cover loosely covers a boutique-style tissue box; Tray is 10¾" x 14" x 2¾" tall [27.3cm x 35.6cm x 7cm]; Box is 5" x 8¼" x 3¼" tall [12.7cm x 21cm x 8.3cm]

SKILL LEVEL: Average

MATERIALS:
- Eight sheets of 7-mesh plastic canvas
- Velcro® closure (optional)
- #16 medium metallic braid (for amount see Color Key)
- Metallic plastic canvas yarn (for amount see Color Key)
- Worsted-weight or plastic canvas yarn (for amounts see Color Key)

CUTTING INSTRUCTIONS:
A: For Tissue Cover Top, cut one according to graph.
B: For Tissue Cover Sides, cut four 31w x 36h-holes.
C: For Tissue Cover Optional Bottom and Flap, cut one 31w x 31h-holes for Bottom and one 31w x 12h-holes for Flap (no graphs).
D: For Tray Bottom and Backing, use two (one for Bottom and one for Backing) 90w x 70h-hole sheets.
E: For Tray Sides and Linings, cut four (two for Sides and two for Linings) according to graph.
F: For Tray Ends and Linings, cut four (two for Ends and two for Linings) according to graph.
G: For Box Lid Top, cut one 54w x 32h-holes.
H: For Box Lid Sides, cut two 54w x 9h-holes.
I: For Box Lid Ends, cut two 32w x 9h-holes.
J: For Box Sides, cut two 52w x 20h-holes.
K: For Box Ends, cut two 30w x 20h-holes.
L: For Box Bottom, cut one 52w x 30h-holes (no graph).

STITCHING INSTRUCTIONS:
NOTE: C and Backing D pieces are not worked.

1: Using colors and stitches indicated, work A, B, Bottom D and E-K pieces according to graphs and work L according to Box Bottom Stitch Pattern Guide; with gold braid, overcast cutout edges of A.

2: Using metallic braid and woody green, embroider detail on B and G pieces as indicated on graphs.

3: With rosewine, whipstitch B pieces wrong sides together; with woody green, whipstitch A to Assembly, forming Cover. For Optional Bottom, with rosewine, whipstitch C pieces together and to one Cover Side according to Optional Tissue Cover Bottom Assembly Illustration on page 63; overcast unfinished edges. Glue closure to Flap and inside Cover (see illustration).

4: For Tray, whipstitch D-F pieces together as indicated and according to Tray Assembly Diagram on page 64.

5: With rosewine, whipstitch J and K pieces wrong sides together and to L as indicated, forming Box. Whipstitch H and I pieces wrong sides together and to G as indicated, forming Box Lid. With woody green, overcast unfinished edges of Box and Box Lid.

COLOR KEY
Dad's Stuff

#16 METALLIC BRAID		KREINIK
■	Gold 80 yds. [73.2m]	#002

METALLIC PC7 YARN		RAINBOW GALLERY
▨	Gold 5 yds. [4.6m]	#01

WORSTED-WEIGHT		WINTUK®
▨	Rosewine 6 oz. [170.1g]	#3032
▨	Woody Green 4 oz. [113.4g]	#3018

B – Tissue Cover Side
(31w x 36h-hole pieces)
Cut 4 & work.

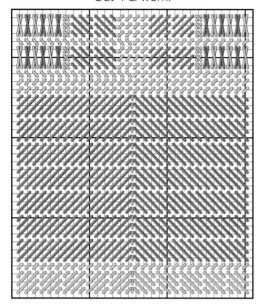

A – Tissue Cover Top
(31w x 31h-hole piece)
Cut 1 & work.

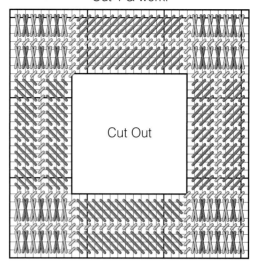

Cut Out

Box Bottom Stitch Pattern Guide

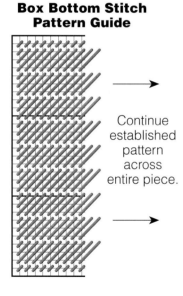

Continue established pattern across entire piece.

K – Box End
(30w x 20h-hole pieces) Cut 2 & work.

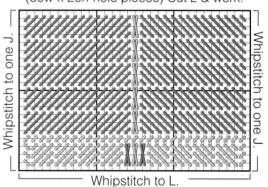

Whipstitch to one J.

Whipstitch to one J.

Whipstitch to L.

I – Box Lid End
(32w x 9h-hole pieces) Cut 2 & work.

Whipstitch to G.

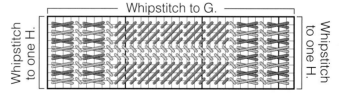

Whipstitch to one H.

Whipstitch to one H.

H – Box Lid Side
(54w x 9h-hole pieces) Cut 2 & work.

Whipstitch to G.

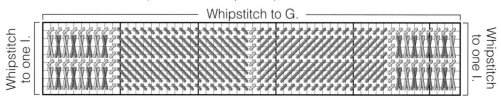

Whipstitch to one I.

Whipstitch to one I.

D – Tray Bottom and Backing

(90w x 70h-hole pieces) Use 2 sheets; work 1 for Bottom & leave 1 unworked for Backing.

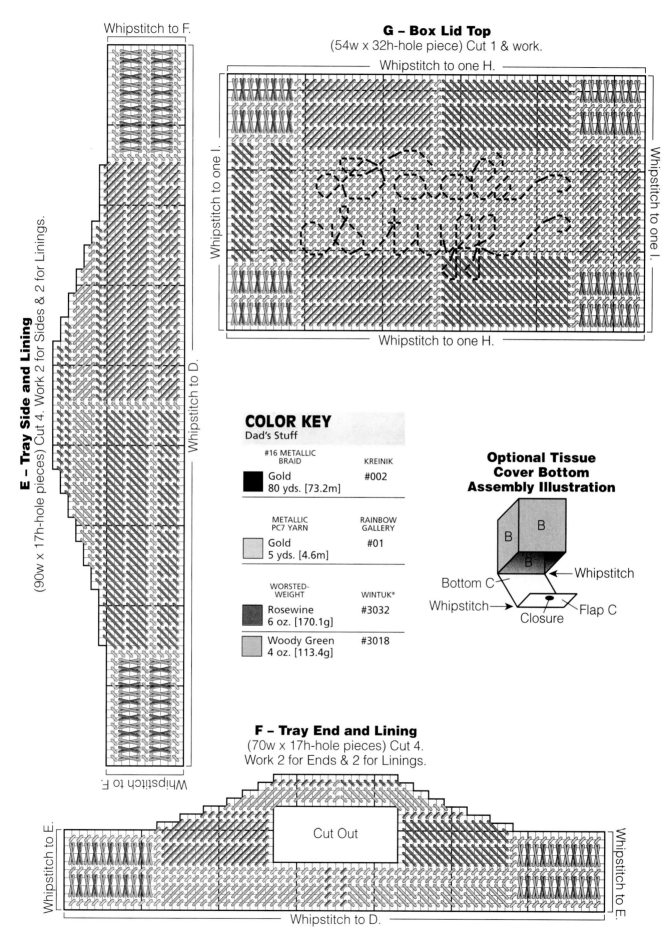

Whipstitch to F.

G – Box Lid Top
(54w x 32h-hole piece) Cut 1 & work.

— Whipstitch to one H. —

Whipstitch to one I.

Whipstitch to one I.

— Whipstitch to one H. —

E – Tray Side and Lining
(90w x 17h-hole pieces) Cut 4. Work 2 for Sides & 2 for Linings.

Whipstitch to D.

COLOR KEY
Dad's Stuff

	#16 METALLIC BRAID	KREINIK
■	Gold 80 yds. [73.2m]	#002

	METALLIC PC7 YARN	RAINBOW GALLERY
▨	Gold 5 yds. [4.6m]	#01

	WORSTED-WEIGHT	WINTUK®
▨	Rosewine 6 oz. [170.1g]	#3032
▨	Woody Green 4 oz. [113.4g]	#3018

Optional Tissue Cover Bottom Assembly Illustration

B

B

B

Bottom C

Whipstitch

Whipstitch

Closure

Flap C

Whipstitch to F.

F – Tray End and Lining
(70w x 17h-hole pieces) Cut 4.
Work 2 for Ends & 2 for Linings.

Whipstitch to E.

Cut Out

Whipstitch to E.

— Whipstitch to D. —

Tray Assembly Diagram
(Pieces are shown in different colors for contrast; gray denotes wrong side.)

Step 1:
Holding one Lining to wrong side of each corresponding Side & End, with woody green, whipstitch short edges of E & F pieces together through all thicknesses.

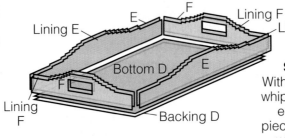

Lining E · E · F · Lining F · Lining E · Bottom D · E · F · Lining F · Backing D

Step 3:
With gold braid, whipstitch cutout edges of F pieces together; with woody green, whipstitch unfinished top edges together.

Step 2:
Holding Backing D to wrong side of Bottom D, whipstitch D pieces to Side & End Assembly through all thicknesses.

COLOR KEY
Dad's Stuff

	#16 METALLIC BRAID	KREINIK
■	Gold 80 yds. [73.2m]	#002

	METALLIC PC7 YARN	RAINBOW GALLERY
▨	Gold 5 yds. [4.6m]	#01

	WORSTED-WEIGHT	WINTUK®
■	Rosewine 6 oz. [170.1g]	#3032
▨	Woody Green 4 oz. [113.4g]	#3018

J – Box Side
(52w x 20h-hole pieces) Cut 2 & work.

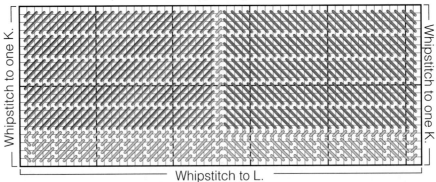

Whipstitch to one K.

Whipstitch to one K.

Whipstitch to L.

Fourth of July!

Create a star-spangled, red, white and blue decor this holiday by stitching these dynamic patriotic projects.

Americana Picnic Set

Designed by Ruby Thacker

Have fun American-style with this stars and stripes picnic setting.

SIZES: Each Place Mat is 12" x 17½" [30.5cm x 44.5cm]; Napkin Holder is 2" x 10½" x 5" tall [5.1 x 26.7cm x 12.7cm]

SKILL LEVEL: Average

MATERIALS:
- Two 12" x 18" [30.5cm x 45.7cm] oval place mat shapes
- 1½ sheets of 7-mesh plastic canvas
- ⅛" [3mm] metallic ribbon (for amount see Color Key)
- Worsted-weight or plastic canvas yarn (for amounts see Color Key)

CUTTING INSTRUCTIONS:
A: For Place Mats, use two oval place mat shapes.
B: For Holder Sides, cut two according to graph.
C: For Holder Ends #1, cut two 12w x 33h-holes.
D: For Holder Ends #2, cut two 13w x 9h-holes.
E: For Holder Bottom, cut one 69w x 13h-holes.

STITCHING INSTRUCTIONS:
NOTE: E is not worked

1: Using colors and stitches indicated, work A-D pieces according to graphs; omitting attachment areas, with matching colors, overcast edges of A-D pieces.

2: With matching colors, whipstitch A-E pieces together as indicated on graphs, forming Holder.

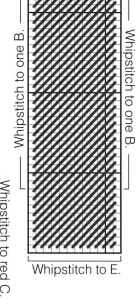

C – Holder End #1
(12w x 33h-hole pieces)
Cut 2. Work 1; substituting
red for dark royal, work 1.

Whipstitch to one B.

Whipstitch to one B.

Whipstitch to E.

ATTACHMENT KEY
☐ End #1/Bottom

B – Holder Side
(69w x 33h-hole pieces) Cut 2. Work 1; substituting
red for dark royal and dark royal for red, work 1.

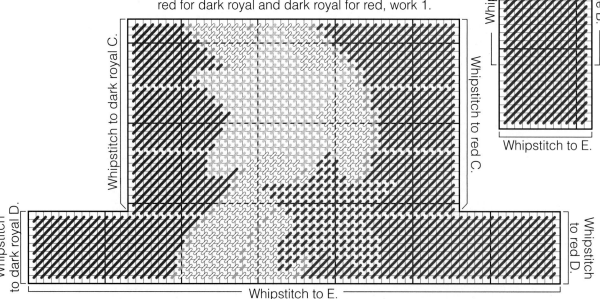

Whipstitch to dark royal C.

Whipstitch to red C.

Whipstitch to dark royal D.

Whipstitch to red D.

Whipstitch to E.

E – Holder Bottom
(69w x 13h-hole piece) Cut 1 & leave unworked.

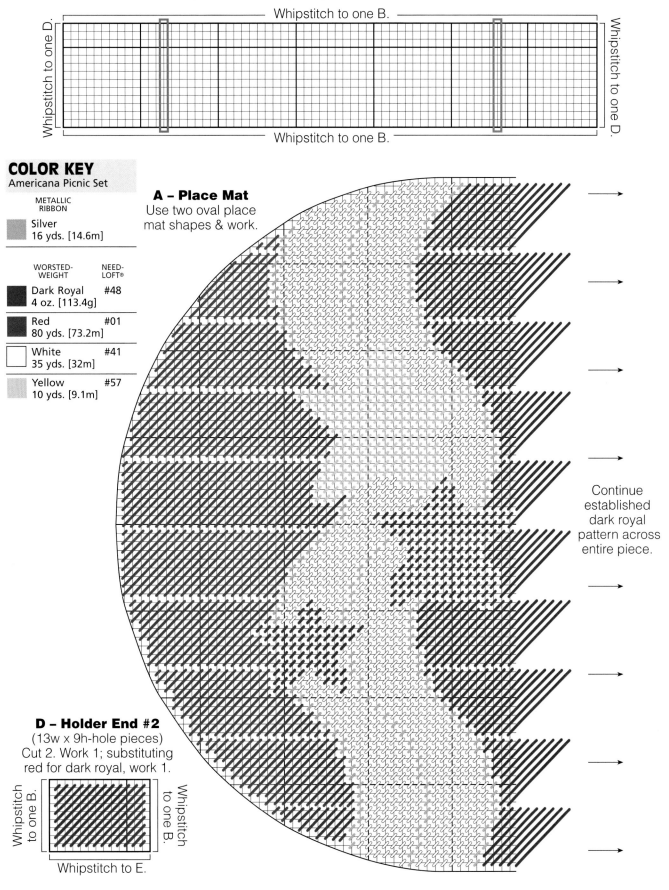

COLOR KEY
Americana Picnic Set

METALLIC RIBBON		
	Silver	16 yds. [14.6m]

WORSTED-WEIGHT	NEED-LOFT®	
Dark Royal	#48	4 oz. [113.4g]
Red	#01	80 yds. [73.2m]
White	#41	35 yds. [32m]
Yellow	#57	10 yds. [9.1m]

A – Place Mat
Use two oval place mat shapes & work.

Continue established dark royal pattern across entire piece.

D – Holder End #2
(13w x 9h-hole pieces)
Cut 2. Work 1; substituting red for dark royal, work 1.

Whipstitch to one B.

Whipstitch to one B.

Whipstitch to E.

Patriotic Pin

Designed by Pam Bull

Show your American spirit with a flag pin made with 14-mesh canvas.

SIZE: 2" x 4" [5.1cm x 10.2cm]

SKILL LEVEL: Average

MATERIALS:
- Scrap piece of ivory 14-mesh plastic canvas
- One 1¼" [3.2cm] bar pin
- Shiny ivory fabric paint
- Craft glue or glue gun
- Six-strand embroidery floss (for amounts see Color Key)

CUTTING INSTRUCTIONS:
A: For Bar, cut one 19w x 5h-holes.
B: For Flags, cut three 19w x 13h-holes.

STITCHING INSTRUCTIONS:
1: Using colors and stitches indicated, work pieces according to graphs; with dk. red for Bar and ultra vy. lt. tan for Flags, overcast edges of pieces.

2: Cut one each 1" [2.5cm], 1½" [3.8cm] and 2" [5.1cm] lengths of ultra vy. lt. tan; position and glue one end of each length to wrong side of Bar and remaining end of each length to wrong side of one Flag as shown in photo.

3: Paint stars on each Flag as shown; glue wrong side of Bar to bar pin.

COLOR KEY
Patriotic Pin

	EMBROIDERY FLOSS	DMC®
	Ultra Vy. Lt. Tan 15 yds. [13.7m]	#739
	Dk. Red 10 yds. [9.1m]	#498
	Vy. Dk. Antique Blue 5 yds. [4.6m]	#3750

A – Bar
(19w x 5h-hole piece)
Cut 1 & work.

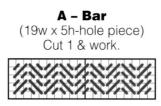

B – Flag
(19w x 13h-hole pieces)
Cut 3 & work.

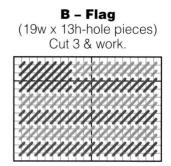

Uncle Sam

Designed by Eunice Asberry

Uncle Sam wants you to have a great Independence Day.

SIZE: 6" x 12½" [15.2cm x 31.8cm]

MATERIALS:
- One sheet of 7-mesh plastic canvas
- Four ¾" [19mm] brads
- Worsted-weight or plastic canvas yarn (for amounts see Color Key)

SKILL LEVEL: Average

CUTTING INSTRUCTIONS:
A: For Body, cut one according to graph.
B: For Arms #1 and #2, cut one each according to graphs.
C: For Legs, cut two according to graph.

STITCHING INSTRUCTIONS:
1: Using colors indicated and continental stitch, work pieces according to graphs; with matching colors, overcast edges of pieces.

2: Using colors (Separate into individual plies, if desired.) and embroidery stitches indicated, embroider detail on A as indicated on graph.

3: Inserting brads through indicated u holes, assemble A-C pieces as shown in photo.

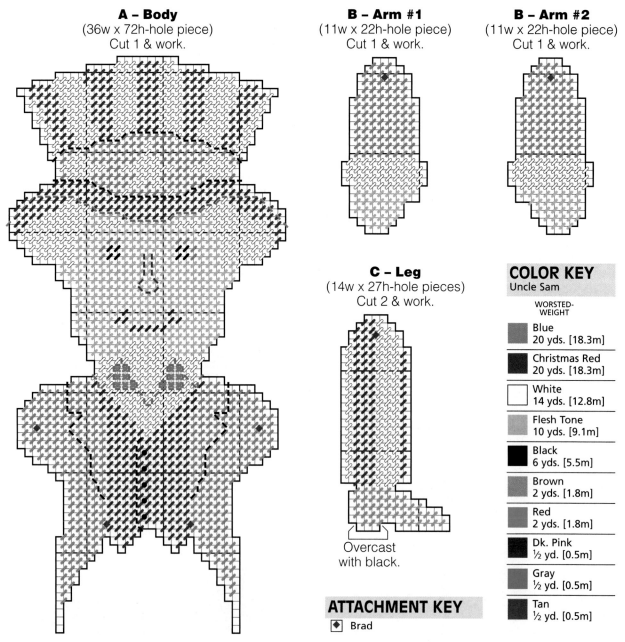

A – Body
(36w x 72h-hole piece)
Cut 1 & work.

B – Arm #1
(11w x 22h-hole piece)
Cut 1 & work.

B – Arm #2
(11w x 22h-hole piece)
Cut 1 & work.

C – Leg
(14w x 27h-hole pieces)
Cut 2 & work.

Overcast with black.

COLOR KEY
Uncle Sam

WORSTED-WEIGHT

Blue	20 yds. [18.3m]
Christmas Red	20 yds. [18.3m]
White	14 yds. [12.8m]
Flesh Tone	10 yds. [9.1m]
Black	6 yds. [5.5m]
Brown	2 yds. [1.8m]
Red	2 yds. [1.8m]
Dk. Pink	½ yd. [0.5m]
Gray	½ yd. [0.5m]
Tan	½ yd. [0.5m]

ATTACHMENT KEY
◆ Brad

American Décor

Designed by Ruby Thacker

Show your patriotic colors with a red, white and blue frame and tissue cover.

SIZES: Tissue Cover loosely covers a boutique-style tissue box; Frame is 3¼" x 8¼" x 8¾" [8.3cm x 21cm x 22.2cm] with a 4⅜" x 5⅛" [11.1cm x 13cm] window opening

SKILL LEVEL: Average

MATERIALS:
• Three sheets of 7-mesh plastic canvas
• Velcro® closure (optional)
• Craft glue or glue gun
• Six-strand metallic embroidery floss (for amount see Color Key)
• Worsted-weight or plastic canvas yarn (for amounts see Color Key)

CUTTING INSTRUCTIONS:
A: For Tissue Cover Top, cut one according to graph.
B: For Tissue Cover Sides, cut four 34w x 37h-holes.
C: For Tissue Cover Optional Bottom and Flap, cut one 34w x 34h-holes for Bottom and one 34w x 12h-holes for Flap (no graphs).
D: For Frame Front, cut one according to graph.
E: For Frame Backing, cut one 54w x 50h-holes (no graph).
F: For Frame Stand, cut one according to graph.

STITCHING INSTRUCTIONS:
NOTE: C, E and F pieces are not worked.

1: Using colors indicated and continental stitch, work A, B and D pieces according to graphs; with dark royal, overcast cutout edges of A and D pieces.

2: Using six strands floss and embroidery stitches indicated, embroider detail on A, B, and D pieces as indicated on graphs.

3: With red, whipstitch A and B pieces wrong sides together, forming Cover. For Optional Bottom, with red, whipstitch C pieces together and to one Cover Side according to Optional Tissue Cover Bottom Assembly Illustration; overcast unfinished edges. Glue closure to Flap and inside Cover (see illustration).

4: For Frame, center Frame Stand on Frame Backing and matching bottom edges, with six strands floss, whipstitch Stand to Backing as indicated; with red, whipstitch Backing to wrong side of Frame Front as indicated. Overcast unfinished top edges of Frame Front.

B – Tissue Cover Side
(34w x 37h-hole pieces)
Cut 4 & work.

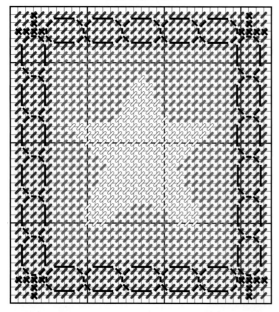

A – Tissue Cover Top
(34w x 34h-hole piece)
Cut 1 & work.

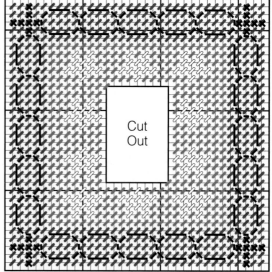

D – Frame Front
(54w x 57h-hole piece) Cut 1 & work.

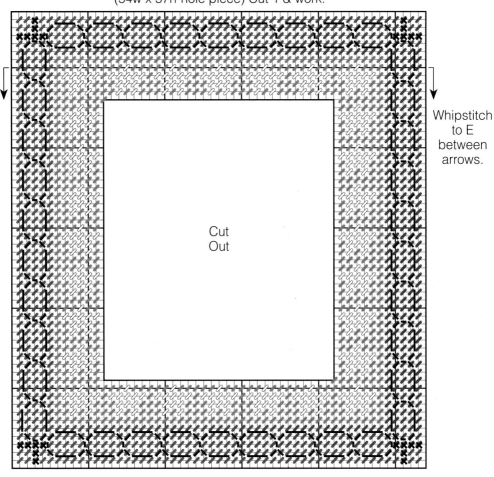

Cut Out

Whipstitch to E between arrows.

F – Frame Stand
(20w x 36h-hole piece)
Cut 1 & leave unworked.

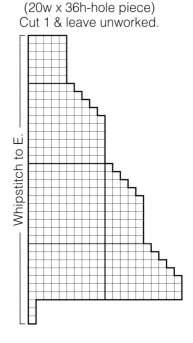

Whipstitch to E.

COLOR KEY
American Decor

EMBROIDERY FLOSS	DMC®
■ Gold 50 yds. [45.7m]	#5282

WORSTED-WEIGHT	NEED-LOFT®
■ Red 50 yds. [45.7m]	#01
■ Dark Royal 38 yds. [34.7m]	#48
□ White 18 yds. [16.5m]	#41

Optional Tissue Cover Bottom Assembly Illustration

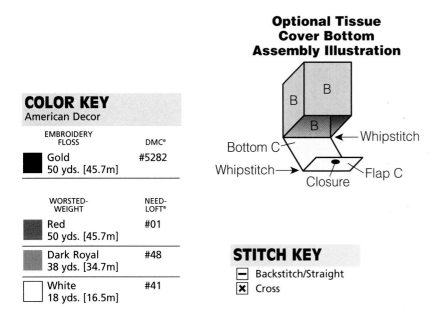

Bottom C
Whipstitch
Whipstitch
Closure
Flap C

STITCH KEY
−	Backstitch/Straight
☒	Cross

Fourth of July Set

Christina Laws and Cynthia Roberts

Add sparks to your celebration with this dynamite holiday set.

SIZES: Each Coaster is 4¾" x 5½" [12.1cm x 14cm]; Coaster Holder is 2½" x 6" x 2½" tall [6.4cm x 15.2cm x 6.4cm]; Candleholder is 4" x 4" x 3½" tall [10.2cm x 10.2cm x 8.9cm]; Frame is 7⅝" x 5½" tall [19.4cm x 14cm] with two 1¾" x 2⅜" [4.4cm x 6cm] photo windows

SKILL LEVEL: Average

MATERIALS:
• Three sheets of 7-mesh plastic canvas
• Craft glue or glue gun
• Worsted-weight or plastic canvas yarn
  (for amounts see Color Key)

CUTTING INSTRUCTIONS:
A: For Coaster Fronts and Backings, cut eight (four for Fronts and four for Backings) according to graph.
B: For Coaster Holder Sides, cut two 38w x 16h-holes.
C: For Coaster Holder Ends, cut two 15w x 16h-holes.
D: For Coaster Holder Bottom, cut one 38w x 15h-holes (no graph).
E: For Candleholder Sides, cut four according to graph.
F: For Candleholder Bottom, cut one 25w x 25h-holes (no graph).
G: For Star Motifs, cut sixteen according to graph.
H: For Frame Fronts, cut two according to graph.
I: For Frame Backings, cut two 20w x 22h-holes (no graph).

COLOR KEY
Fourth of July Set

WORSTED-
WEIGHT

□ White
56 yds. [51.2m]

■ Red
48 yds. [43.9m]

■ Blue
40 yds. [36.6m]

STITCHING INSTRUCTIONS:
NOTE: Backing A, D, F and I pieces are not worked.

1: Using colors and stitches indicated, work A-C, E, G and H pieces according to graphs; with white, overcast cutout edges of E and H pieces and edges of G pieces.

2: Using white and smyrna cross (See stitch illustration on page 76.), embroider detail on H pieces as indicated on graph.

3: For Coasters (make 4), holding one backing A to wrong side of one Front A, with matching colors as shown in photo, whipstitch together. With matching colors, whipstitch B-D pieces together as indicated, forming Coaster Holder; overcast unfinished edges. Glue three Star Motifs to each Side and one to each End.

4: With matching colors as shown, whipstitch E and F pieces together as indicated, forming Candleholder; overcast unfinished edges. Glue two Star Motifs to each Side as shown.

5: With red, whipstitch H pieces together (see photo); with matching colors, overcast unfinished edges. Leaving top edge open for picture insertion, glue one I to wrong side of each H centered over cutout as indicated.

A – Coaster Front and Backing
(36w x 31h-hole pieces)
Cut 8. Work 4 for Fronts & leave 4
unworked for Backings.

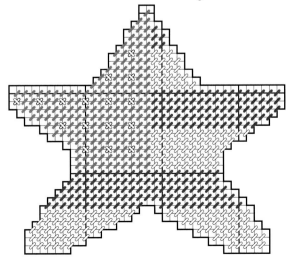

B – Coaster Holder Side
(38w x 16h-hole pieces) Cut 2 & work.

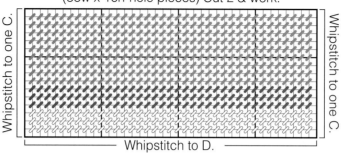

Whipstitch to one C.
Whipstitch to one C.
Whipstitch to D.

G – Star Motif
(9w x 8h-hole pieces)
Cut 16 & work.

COLOR KEY
Fourth of July Set

WORSTED-WEIGHT

☐	White	56 yds. [51.2m]
■	Red	48 yds. [43.9m]
■	Blue	40 yds. [36.6m]

C – Coaster Holder End
(15w x 16h-hole pieces)
Cut 2 & work.

Whipstitch to one B.
Whipstitch to one B.
Whipstitch to D.

Smyrna Cross Stitch Illustration

PLACEMENT KEY
☐ Frame Backing

STITCH KEY
✳ Smyrna Cross

H – Frame Front
(25w x 36h-hole pieces)
Cut 2 & work.

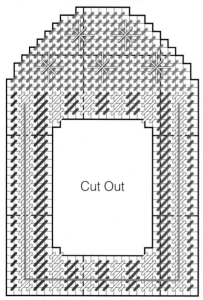

Cut Out

E – Candleholder Side
(25w x 23h-hole pieces)
Cut 4 & work.

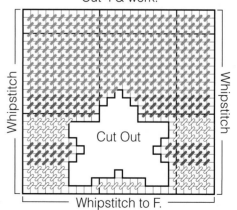

Whipstitch
Whipstitch
Cut Out
Whipstitch to F.

Happy Birthday!

Make birthdays a special day by celebrating with friends and family. Create great party decorations using plastic canvas.

Birthday Cake Box

Designed by Lee Lindeman

Packaging a small birthday surprise is a piece of cake with this pretty box.

SIZE: 3½" x 5½" x 3¼" tall [8.9cm x 14cm x 8.3cm], not including plate

SKILL LEVEL: Average

MATERIALS:
• One sheet of 7-mesh plastic canvas
• One 9" x 12" [22.9cm x 30.5cm] sheet of lilac felt
• One white 8" [20.3cm] salad plate
• Craft glue or glue gun
• Worsted-weight or plastic canvas yarn (for amounts see Color Key)

CUTTING INSTRUCTIONS:
A: For Cake Sides #1 and #2, cut two (one for Side #1 and one for Side #2) 30w x 19h-holes.
B: For Back, cut one 23w x 19h-holes.
C: For Top, cut one according to graph.
D: For Bottom, cut one according to graph.

STITCHING INSTRUCTIONS:
1: Using colors and stitches indicated, work pieces according to graphs.

NOTE: Cut two 12" [30.5cm] lengths of white and one 12" [30.5cm] length of lilac.

2: Using colors indicated and French knots, embroider detail on B and C pieces as indicated on graphs. Glue cut strands of yarn to B and C pieces as indicated, trimming any excess.

NOTE: Using A-D pieces as patterns for Backings, cut one each from felt ⅛" [3mm] smaller at all edges.

3: Glue Felt Backings to wrong side of each corresponding piece.

4: With matching colors as shown in photo, whipstitch A-D pieces wrong sides together as indicated; overcast unfinished edges. Center and glue Cake Box to plate.

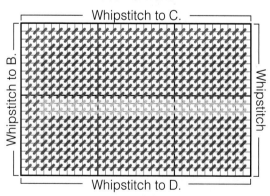

A – Side #1
(30w x 19h-hole piece)
Cut 1 & work.

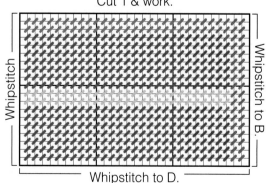

A – Side #2
(30w x 19h-hole piece)
Cut 1 & work.

C – Top
(27w x 27h-hole piece)
Cut 1 & work.

Whipstitch to
A#1 between
arrows.

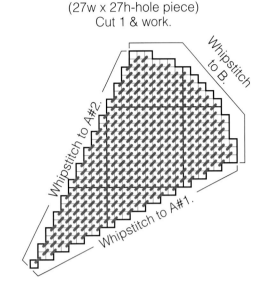

D – Bottom
(27w x 27h-hole piece)
Cut 1 & work.

Whipstitch to B.

Whipstitch to A#2.

Whipstitch to A#1.

B – Back
(23w x 19-h-hole piece)
Cut 1 & work.

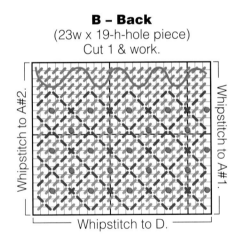

Whipstitch to A#2.

Whipstitch to A#1.

Whipstitch to D.

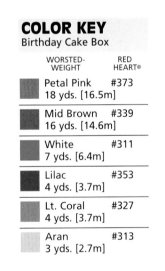

COLOR KEY
Birthday Cake Box

	WORSTED-WEIGHT	RED HEART®
	Petal Pink 18 yds. [16.5m]	#373
	Mid Brown 16 yds. [14.6m]	#339
	White 7 yds. [6.4m]	#311
	Lilac 4 yds. [3.7m]	#353
	Lt. Coral 4 yds. [3.7m]	#327
	Aran 3 yds. [2.7m]	#313

STITCH KEY
 French Knot

PLACEMENT KEY
☐ Lilac Yarn
☐ White Yarn

Happy Birthday Balloons

Designed by Sandra Miller Maxfield

These birthday balloons can be used year after year to honor a special boy or girl.

SIZE: 11" x 13" [27.9cm x 33cm], not including ribbons.

SKILL LEVEL: Average

MATERIALS:
- Two sheets of clear and one sheet of black 7-mesh plastic canvas
- 1½ yds. [1.4m] white ¼" [6mm] curling ribbon
- ½ yd. [0.5m] red ⅞" [22mm] satin ribbon
- One penny (for weight)
- Craft glue or glue gun
- Worsted-weight or plastic canvas yarn (for amounts see Color Key).

CUTTING INSTRUCTIONS:
A: For Balloons, cut three from clear according to graph.
B: For "Happy", cut one from black according to graph.
C: For "Birthday", cut one from black according to graph.

STITCHING INSTRUCTIONS:
1: Using colors and stitches indicated, work pieces according to graphs. With matching colors, overcast edges of A pieces.

NOTE: Cut curling ribbon into three 18" [45.7cm] lengths.

2: Tie one end of one ribbon around neck of each Balloon as shown in photo. Glue Balloons together as shown. Knot ribbons together about 9" [22.9cm] from ends (see photo); curl ends, if desired.

3: Tie red ribbon into a bow; glue bow to knot of white ribbon. Glue penny to wrong side of red bow over knot. Glue "Happy" and "Birthday" to Balloons as desired or as shown. Hang as desired.

COLOR KEY
Happy Birthday Balloons

	WORSTED-WEIGHT	NEED-LOFT®
Red	34 yds. [31.1m]	#01
Royal	32 yds. [29.3m]	#32
Yellow	32 yds. [29.3m]	#57
Fern	3 yds. [2.7m]	#23
Bright Orange	2 yds. [1.8m]	#58
Bright Purple	2 yds. [1.8m]	#64

A – Balloon
(41w x 54h-hole pieces)
Cut 3 from clear. Work 1; substituting royal for yellow, work 1; substituting red for yellow, reverse 1 & work.

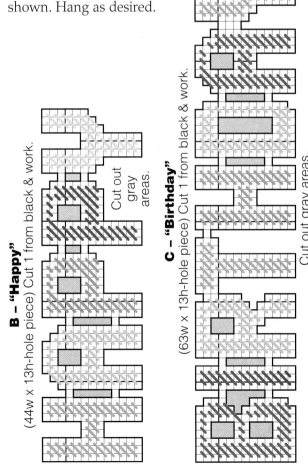

B – "Happy"
(44w x 13h-hole piece) Cut 1 from black & work.
Cut out gray areas.

C – "Birthday"
(63w x 13h-hole piece) Cut 1 from black & work.
Cut out gray areas.

Happy Halloween!

It's treats you get when you create frightful decorations and party favors for the many ghosts and goblins sure to come your way.

Haunted House

Designed by Nancy Dorman

Set your table or sideboard with this fabulously creepy haunted house.

SIZE: 5½" x 8½" x 6¼" tall [14cm x 21.6cm x 15.9cm]

SKILL LEVEL: Challenging

MATERIALS:
- Two sheets of clear 7-mesh plastic canvas
- Scrap of black 7-mesh plastic canvas
- ¼ sheet of clear 10-mesh plastic canvas
- Small amount of Spanish moss
- Four small orange artificial leaves
- Small amount of polyester fiberfill
- Craft glue or glue gun
- Six-strand embroidery floss (for amounts see Color Key)
- Worsted-weight or plastic canvas yarn (for amounts see Color Key)

CUTTING INSTRUCTIONS:
A: For House Front, cut one from clear 7-mesh according to graph.
B: For House Back, cut one from clear 7-mesh 39w x 22h-holes.
C: For House Sides, cut two from clear 7-mesh according to graph.
D: For House Roof Front, cut one from clear 7-mesh according to graph.
E: For House Roof Back, cut one from clear 7-mesh 43w x 23h-holes.
F: For Gable Roof, cut two from clear 7-mesh according to graph.
G: For Balcony Floor, cut one from clear 7-mesh 22w x 3h-holes.
H: For Porch Posts, cut one from black 7-mesh according to graph.
I: For Balcony Railing, cut one from black 7-mesh according to graph.
J: For Large Shutters #1 and #2, cut six each from clear 7-mesh according to graphs.
K: For Small Shutters #1 and #2, cut three each from clear 7-mesh according to graphs.

L: For Base, cut one from clear 7-mesh according to graph.
M: For Sign, cut one from 10-mesh according to graph.
N: For Ghost, cut one from 10-mesh according to graph.
O: For Tombstones, cut two from 10-mesh according to graph.
P: For Large Pumpkin, cut one from 10-mesh according to graph.
Q: For Small Pumpkin, cut one from 10-mesh according to graph.

STITCHING INSTRUCTIONS:
NOTES: H and I pieces are not worked.
Separate 4-ply yarn into 2 strands for stitching on 10-mesh canvas.

1: Using colors and stitches indicated, work A-G and J-Q pieces according to graphs; omitting attachment areas, with dk. gray for cutouts, tan for small pumpkin stems and with matching colors, overcast A-G and J-Q pieces.

2: Using six strands floss and yarn (Separate into individual plies if desired.) in colors and embroidery stitches indicated, embroider detail on A-C and M, O and Q pieces as indicated on graphs.

3: Using herringbone whipstitch, whipstitch and assemble A-I pieces as indicated and according to House Assembly Diagram on page 86.

4: Glue Shutters, Sign, Ghost, Tombstones, Pumpkins and artificial leaves to House and Base as shown in photo or as desired. Carefully pull apart fiberfill to form cobwebs; glue cobwebs and Spanish moss to House and Base as shown or as desired.

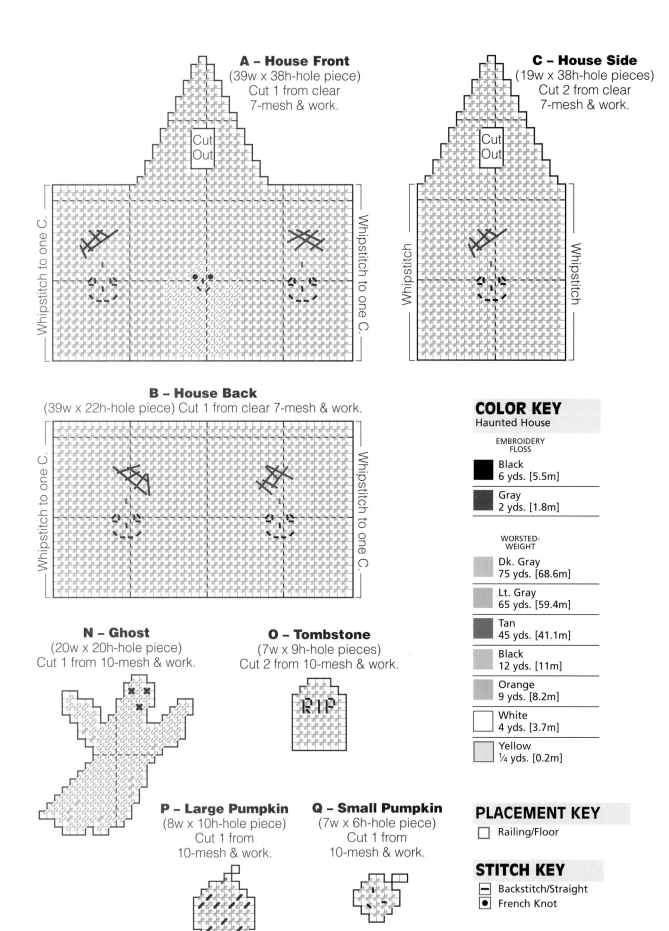

A – House Front
(39w x 38h-hole piece)
Cut 1 from clear
7-mesh & work.

Cut Out

Whipstitch to one C.

Whipstitch to one C.

C – House Side
(19w x 38h-hole pieces)
Cut 2 from clear
7-mesh & work.

Cut Out

Whipstitch

Whipstitch

B – House Back
(39w x 22h-hole piece) Cut 1 from clear 7-mesh & work.

Whipstitch to one C.

Whipstitch to one C.

N – Ghost
(20w x 20h-hole piece)
Cut 1 from 10-mesh & work.

O – Tombstone
(7w x 9h-hole pieces)
Cut 2 from 10-mesh & work.

RIP

P – Large Pumpkin
(8w x 10h-hole piece)
Cut 1 from
10-mesh & work.

Q – Small Pumpkin
(7w x 6h-hole piece)
Cut 1 from
10-mesh & work.

COLOR KEY
Haunted House

EMBROIDERY FLOSS

■	Black 6 yds. [5.5m]
■	Gray 2 yds. [1.8m]

WORSTED-WEIGHT

■	Dk. Gray 75 yds. [68.6m]
■	Lt. Gray 65 yds. [59.4m]
■	Tan 45 yds. [41.1m]
■	Black 12 yds. [11m]
■	Orange 9 yds. [8.2m]
□	White 4 yds. [3.7m]
■	Yellow ¼ yds. [0.2m]

PLACEMENT KEY
□ Railing/Floor

STITCH KEY
− Backstitch/Straight
• French Knot

D – House Roof Front
(43w x 23h-hole piece) Cut 1 from clear 7-mesh & work.

Whipstitch to E.

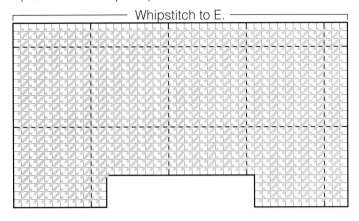

E – House Roof Back
(43w x 23h-hole piece) Cut 1 from clear 7-mesh & work.

Whipstitch to D.

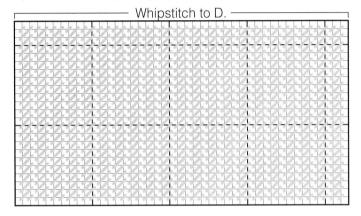

J – Large Shutter #1
(3w x 10h-hole pieces)
Cut 6 from clear
7-mesh & work.

J – Large Shutter #2
(3w x 10h-hole pieces)
Cut 6 from clear
7-mesh & work.

K – Small Shutter #1
(2w x 5h-hole pieces)
Cut 3 from clear
7-mesh & work.

K – Small Shutter #2
(2w x 5h-hole pieces)
Cut 3 from clear
7-mesh & work.

M – Sign
(20w x 3h-hole piece)
Cut 1 from 10-mesh & work.

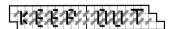

F – Gable Roof
(12w x 20h-hole pieces)
Cut 2 from clear 7-mesh.
Work 1 & 1 reversed.

Whipstitch

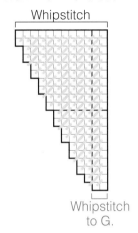

Whipstitch
to G.

G – Balcony Floor
(22w x 3h-hole piece)
Cut 1 from clear 7-mesh & work.

Whipstitch to F.

Whipstitch to F.

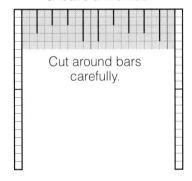

H – Porch Posts
(22w x 20h-hole piece)
Cut 1 from black 7-mesh
& leave unworked.

Cut around bars
carefully.

I – Balcony Railing
(20w x 3h-hole piece)
Cut 1 from black 7-mesh
& leave unworked.

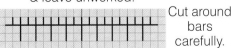

Cut around
bars
carefully.

L – Base
(55w x 55h-hole piece)
Cut 1 from clear
7-mesh & work.

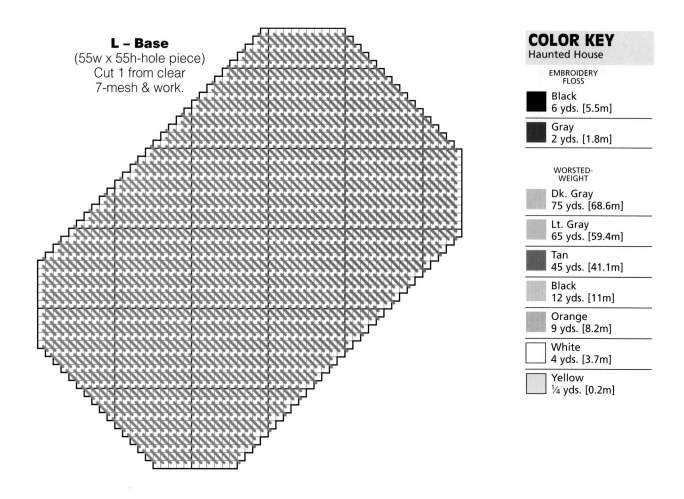

COLOR KEY
Haunted House

EMBROIDERY
FLOSS

■	Black 6 yds. [5.5m]
■	Gray 2 yds. [1.8m]

WORSTED-
WEIGHT

	Dk. Gray 75 yds. [68.6m]
	Lt. Gray 65 yds. [59.4m]
	Tan 45 yds. [41.1m]
	Black 12 yds. [11m]
	Orange 9 yds. [8.2m]
□	White 4 yds. [3.7m]
	Yellow ¼ yds. [0.2m]

House Assembly Diagram
(Pieces are shown in different colors
for contrast; gray denotes wrong side.)

Step 1:
With lt. gray, whipstitch
A-C pieces wrong sides
together; center & glue
to right side of L.

Step 2:
With dk. gray, whipstitch
D & E pieces wrong
sides together leaving
House Roof Back
unattached for opening;
glue House Roof Front to
top edge of House Front
& one edge of Side
pieces.

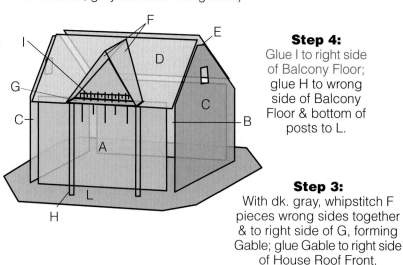

Step 4:
Glue I to right side
of Balcony Floor;
glue H to wrong
side of Balcony
Floor & bottom of
posts to L.

Step 3:
With dk. gray, whipstitch F
pieces wrong sides together
& to right side of G, forming
Gable; glue Gable to right side
of House Roof Front.

Monster Treat Box

Designed by Janelle Giese of Janelle Marie Designs

This tricky guy will be happy to hand out treats this Halloween.

SIZE: 4" x 5½" x 9¾" tall [10.2cm x 14cm x 24.8cm]

SKILL LEVEL: Challenging

MATERIALS:
- ½ sheet of clear 7-mesh plastic canvas
- One sheet of orange 7-mesh plastic canvas
- Craft glue or glue gun
- No. 3 pearl cotton (for amount see Color Key)
- Heavy (#32) glow-in-the-dark metallic braid (for amount see Color Key)
- Worsted weight or plastic canvas yarn (for amounts see Color Key)

CUTTING INSTRUCTIONS:
A: For Motif, cut one from clear according to graph.
B: For Box Sides, cut four from orange according to graph.
C: For Box Bottom, cut one from orange 25w x 25h-holes (no graph).

STITCHING INSTRUCTIONS:
NOTE: B and C pieces are not worked.

1: Using colors and stitches indicated, work A according to graph; with matching colors as shown in photo, overcast edges.

2: Using pearl cotton or six strands floss, braid and yarn (Separate into individual plies, if desired.) in colors and embroidery stitches indicated, embroider detail on A as indicated on graph.

3: With bittersweet, whipstitch B and C pieces together, forming Box; do not overcast unfinished edges. Matching bottom edges, glue Motif to one Side.

B – Box Side
(25w x 35h-hole pieces)
Cut 4 from orange & leave unworked.

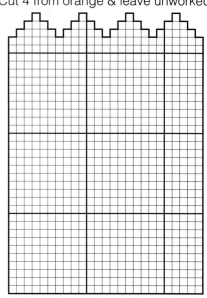

STITCH KEY
- ▬ Backstitch/Straight
- ● French Knot

A – Motif
(36w x 65h-hole piece)
Cut 1 from clear & work.

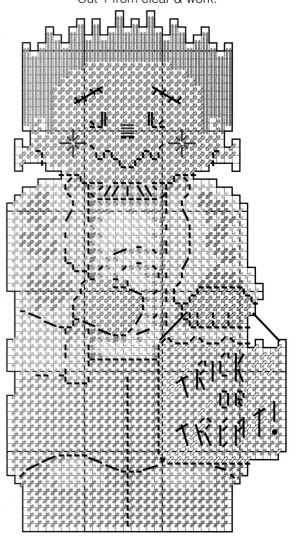

COLOR KEY
Monster Treat Box

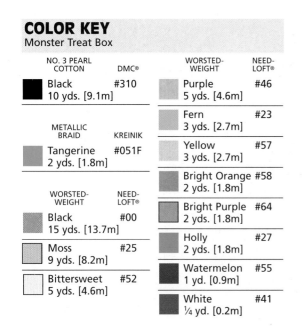

NO. 3 PEARL COTTON	DMC®
■ Black 10 yds. [9.1m]	#310

METALLIC BRAID	KREINIK
Tangerine 2 yds. [1.8m]	#051F

WORSTED-WEIGHT	NEED-LOFT®
Black 15 yds. [13.7m]	#00
Moss 9 yds. [8.2m]	#25
Bittersweet 5 yds. [4.6m]	#52

WORSTED-WEIGHT	NEED-LOFT®
Purple 5 yds. [4.6m]	#46
Fern 3 yds. [2.7m]	#23
Yellow 3 yds. [2.7m]	#57
Bright Orange 2 yds. [1.8m]	#58
Bright Purple 2 yds. [1.8m]	#64
Holly 2 yds. [1.8m]	#27
Watermelon 1 yd. [0.9m]	#55
White ¼ yd. [0.2m]	#41

Batty Belfry

Designed by Janelle Giese of Janelle Marie Designs

Beware! This vampire is ready to treat your tricksters this holiday.

SIZE: 7" x 13" [17.8cm x 33cm], not including hanger

SKILL LEVEL: Average

MATERIALS:
- One sheet of 7-mesh plastic canvas
- Three ½" [13mm] silver liberty bells
- Twelve 7mm silver jump rings
- ⅓ yd. [0.3m] 2mm silver chain
- No. 3 pearl cotton (for amount see Color Key)
- Heavy (#32) glow-in-the-dark metallic braid (for amount see Color Key)
- Worsted weight or plastic canvas yarn (for amounts see Color Key)

CUTTING INSTRUCTIONS:
A: For Vampire, cut one according to graph.
B: For Bat, cut one according to graph.

STITCHING INSTRUCTIONS:
1: Using colors and stitches indicated, work pieces according to graphs; with matching colors as shown in photo, overcast edges of pieces.

2: Using pearl cotton or six strands floss, braid and yarn (Separate into individual plies, if desired.) in colors and embroidery stitches indicated, embroider detail on A as indicated on graph.

NOTE: Cut chain into one 8" [20.3cm], three 1" [2.5cm], and two ½" [1.3cm] lengths.

3: Insert one jump ring in each ◆ hole on A and B pieces as indicated. Attach one end of 8" length to each jump ring at top of Vampire for hanger. Attach one end of each of two 1" chains to jump rings at bottom of Vampire (see photo) and remaining end of each chain to one jump ring at top of Bat (see photo).

4: Attach one end of remaining chains to jump rings at bottom of Bat as shown and remaining jump rings and liberty bells to remaining ends of chains (see photo). Hang as desired.

ATTACHMENT KEY
◆ Jump Ring

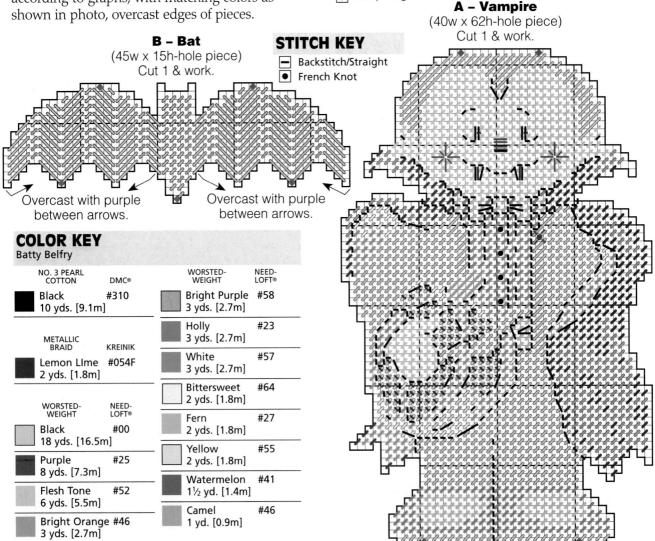

B – Bat
(45w x 15h-hole piece)
Cut 1 & work.

Overcast with purple between arrows.

Overcast with purple between arrows.

STITCH KEY
— Backstitch/Straight
● French Knot

A – Vampire
(40w x 62h-hole piece)
Cut 1 & work.

COLOR KEY
Batty Belfry

NO. 3 PEARL COTTON	DMC®		WORSTED-WEIGHT	NEED-LOFT®
■ Black 10 yds. [9.1m]	#310		▨ Bright Purple 3 yds. [2.7m]	#58
			▨ Holly 3 yds. [2.7m]	#23
METALLIC BRAID	**KREINIK**		▨ White 3 yds. [2.7m]	#57
■ Lemon LIme 2 yds. [1.8m]	#054F		▨ Bittersweet 2 yds. [1.8m]	#64
			▨ Fern 2 yds. [1.8m]	#27
WORSTED-WEIGHT	**NEED-LOFT®**		▨ Yellow 2 yds. [1.8m]	#55
▨ Black 18 yds. [16.5m]	#00		▨ Watermelon 1½ yd. [1.4m]	#41
▨ Purple 8 yds. [7.3m]	#25		▨ Camel 1 yd. [0.9m]	#46
▨ Flesh Tone 6 yds. [5.5m]	#52			
▨ Bright Orange 3 yds. [2.7m]	#46			

Halloween Bear

Designed by Kathleen Hurley

Greet your goblins with a cute peek-a-boo bear.

SIZE: 8" x 11½" [20.3cm x 29.2cm]

SKILL LEVEL: Easy

MATERIALS:
- One sheet of 7-mesh plastic canvas
- Craft glue or glue gun
- No. 3 pearl cotton or six-strand embroidery floss (for amounts see Color Key)
- Worsted-weight or plastic canvas yarn (for amounts see Color Key)

CUTTING INSTRUCTIONS:

A: For Bear and Pumpkin, cut one according to graph.
B: For Leaves, cut four according to graph.

STITCHING INSTRUCTIONS:

1: Using colors indicated and continental stitch, work pieces according to graphs. With bittersweet for pumpkin areas (see photo) and with matching colors as shown in photo, overcast edges of pieces.

2: Using pearl cotton or six strands floss in colors and embroidery stitches indicated, embroider detail on A as indicated on graph.

3: Glue Leaves to Bear and Pumpkin as shown. Hang as desired.

STITCH KEY
- ⊟ Backstitch/Straight
- ⊙ French Knot

A – Bear and Pumpkin
(46w x 70h-hole piece)
Cut 1 & work.

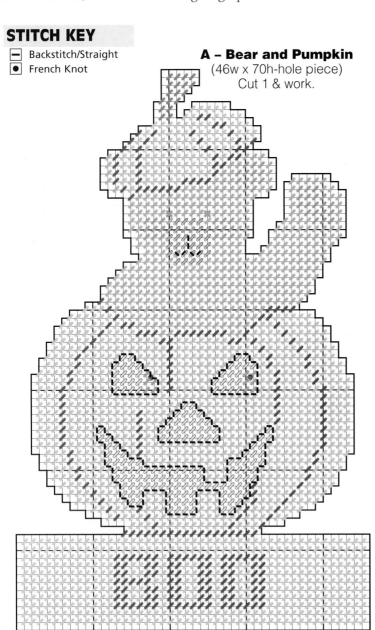

B – Leaf
(14w x 15h-hole pieces)
Cut 4 & work.

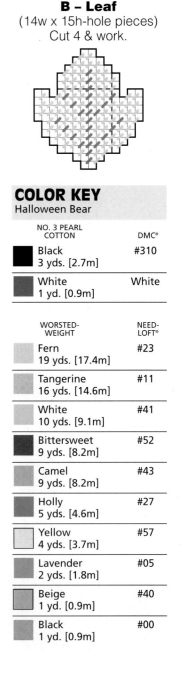

COLOR KEY
Halloween Bear

	NO. 3 PEARL COTTON	DMC®
■	Black 3 yds. [2.7m]	#310
■	White 1 yd. [0.9m]	White

	WORSTED-WEIGHT	NEED-LOFT®
	Fern 19 yds. [17.4m]	#23
	Tangerine 16 yds. [14.6m]	#11
	White 10 yds. [9.1m]	#41
	Bittersweet 9 yds. [8.2m]	#52
	Camel 9 yds. [8.2m]	#43
	Holly 5 yds. [4.6m]	#27
	Yellow 4 yds. [3.7m]	#57
	Lavender 2 yds. [1.8m]	#05
	Beige 1 yd. [0.9m]	#40
	Black 1 yd. [0.9m]	#00

Haunted Tree

Designed by Irma Sippley

Ghosts and goblins will feel right at home when they see this haunted tree.

SIZE: 14¼" x 16½" [36.2cm x 41.9cm]

SKILL LEVEL: Easy

MATERIALS:
- One 13½" x 21½" [34.3cm x 57.2cm] and ½ standard-size sheet of 7-mesh plastic canvas
- Craft glue or glue gun
- Worsted-weight or plastic canvas yarn (for amounts see Color Key)

CUTTING INSTRUCTIONS:

A: For Tree, cut one from large sheet according to graph.

B: For Ghost #1, cut one from standard-size sheet according to graph.

C: For Ghost #2, cut one from standard-size sheet according to graph.

STITCHING INSTRUCTIONS:

1: Using colors indicated and continental stitch, work pieces according to graphs; with matching colors as shown in photo, overcast edges of pieces.

2: Glue Ghosts #1 and #2 to Tree as shown or as desired. Hang or display as desired.

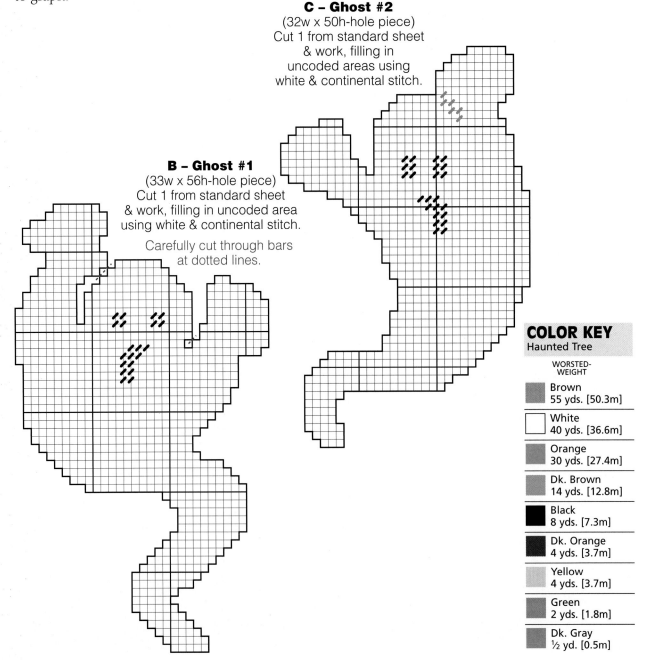

C – Ghost #2
(32w x 50h-hole piece)
Cut 1 from standard sheet
& work, filling in
uncoded areas using
white & continental stitch.

B – Ghost #1
(33w x 56h-hole piece)
Cut 1 from standard sheet
& work, filling in uncoded area
using white & continental stitch.

Carefully cut through bars
at dotted lines.

COLOR KEY
Haunted Tree

WORSTED-WEIGHT

■	Brown 55 yds. [50.3m]
□	White 40 yds. [36.6m]
■	Orange 30 yds. [27.4m]
■	Dk. Brown 14 yds. [12.8m]
■	Black 8 yds. [7.3m]
■	Dk. Orange 4 yds. [3.7m]
■	Yellow 4 yds. [3.7m]
■	Green 2 yds. [1.8m]
■	Dk. Gray ½ yd. [0.5m]

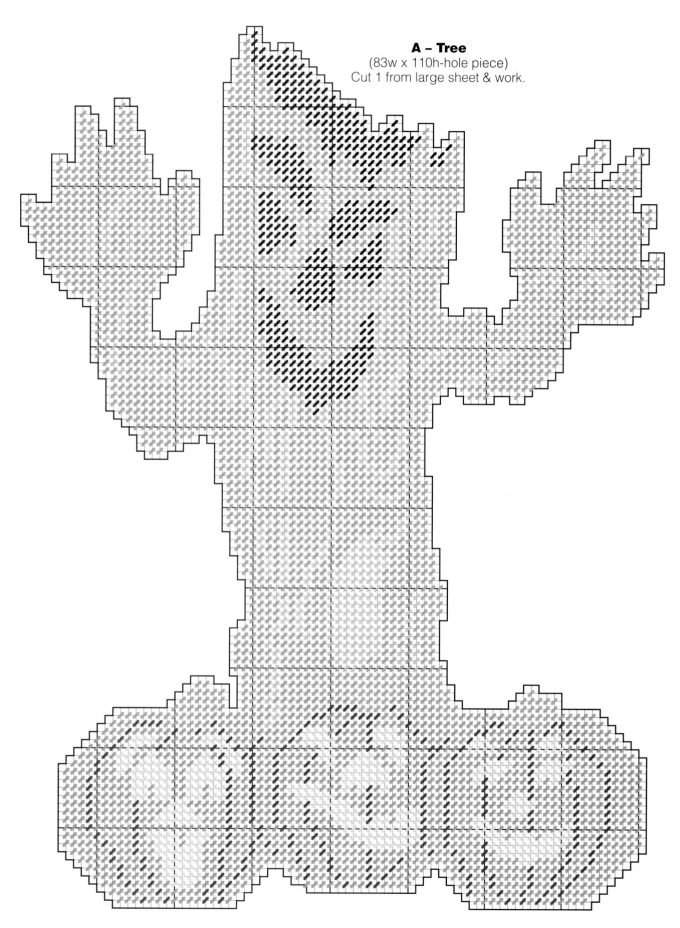

A – Tree
(83w x 110h-hole piece)
Cut 1 from large sheet & work.

Trick or Treat Kitty

Designed by Lee Lindeman

This cool cat is ready for a night of tricks and treats.

SIZE: 6" x 9" [15.2cm x 22.9cm], not including Pumpkin and Basket

SKILL LEVEL: Challenging

MATERIALS:
- One sheet of 7-mesh plastic canvas
- One black 12mm animal nose
- Two brown 10mm animal eyes
- Four black 5mm half round bead eyes
- Scrap pieces of orange, black, white and gray felt or ultrasuede
- Scrap piece of green plastic foam
- 10-yd. [9.1m] spool of silver 18-gauge wire
- 10 yd. [9.1m] spool of green 18-gauge wire
- One ¼" [6mm] and one ⅜" [10mm] dowel rod
- One round toothpick
- ¼" x 4" [0.6cm x 10.2cm] tree branch
- Small amount of orange tissue paper
- Several small wrapped pieces of candy
- Polyester fiberfill
- Sandpaper or steel file
- Craft glue or glue gun
- Six-strand embroidery floss (for amounts see Color Key)
- Worsted-weight or plastic canvas yarn (for amounts see Color Key)

CUTTING INSTRUCTIONS:
A: For Kitty Head Front and Back, cut one each according to graphs.
B: For Kitty Body Front and Back, cut one each according to graphs.
C: For Kitty Hand Fronts and Backs, cut one each according to graphs.
D: For Kitty Foot Tops and Bottoms, cut one each according to graphs.
E: For Kitty Tail Tips, cut two according to graph.
F: For Pumpkin Front and Back, cut one each according to graphs.
G: For Owl Motif, cut one according to graph.
H: For Owl Bag Sides, cut two according to graph.
I: For Owl Bag End, cut one 5w x 28h-holes.

STITCHING INSTRUCTIONS:
1: Using colors indicated and continental stitch, work pieces according to graphs; with matching colors, overcast indicated edges of A-F pieces and edges of G.

2: Using floss and yarn (Separate into individual plies, if desired.) and embroidery stitches (Leave ½" [13mm] loops on modified turkey work stitches.) indicated, embroider detail on Front A, B, E, Front F and G pieces as indicated on graphs. Cut through modified turkey work stitches and fray ends; trim and fray ends as desired.

NOTES: For neck, tightly coil white wire around ⅜" dowel rod until neck is approximately ¾" [19mm] in length.
Remove shank from back of nose; file smooth.

3: For Head, with silver, whipstitch A pieces wrong sides together, stuffing face lightly with fiberfill and securing neck in place (see photo) before closing. For Kitty ears, cut two outer ears from gray felt or ultrasuede and two inner ears from white felt or ultrasuede according to Kitty Ear Patterns; glue one inner ear to each outer ear. Glue ears to right side of Back A (see photo) and animal eyes and nose to Front A as shown.

NOTE: For each arm (make 2), tightly coil silver wire around ¼" dowel rod until arm is approximately 2¾" [7cm] in length; for each leg (make 2), tightly coil silver wire around ¼" dowel until leg is approximately 3¼" [8.3cm] in length; for tail, tightly coil silver wire around ¼" dowel until tail is approximately 4" [10.2cm] in length.

4: With silver, whipstitch B pieces wrong sides together, stuffing Body generously with fiberfill and securing arms, legs and neck in place (see photo) before closing. Whipstitch E pieces wrong sides together, securing one end of tail in place before closing; twist and screw remaining end of Tail into place as indicated on Back B graph.

5: For each Hand (make 2), with silver, whipstitch one Front C and one Back C wrong sides together, securing over end of one arm before closing.

6: For each Foot (make 2), with silver, whipstitch one Top D and one Bottom D wrong sides together, stuffing lightly with fiberfill and securing over end of one leg before closing; embroider detail on each Foot as indicated.

NOTES: For Pumpkin stem, tightly coil green wire around toothpick until stem is approximately 1" [2.5cm] in length.
Cut Pumpkin Collar from green foam according to Pumpkin Collar Pattern.

7: For Pumpkin, with orange, whipstitch F pieces wrong sides together, stuffing lightly with fiberfill and securing top opening over one end of Pumpkin stem (see photo). Center and glue Pumpkin Collar over bottom opening; insert tree branch through hole in Collar and into bottom opening of Pumpkin, gluing to secure. Cut pumpkin nose from black felt or ultrasuede according to Pumpkin Nose Pattern. Glue nose and two half round beads to Front of Pumpkin. Glue tree branch to one Hand and to Kitty's Body as shown.

NOTE: Cut six 2" [5.1cm] lengths of black yarn, one 10" [25.4cm] length of black yarn and one 10" [25.4cm] length of orange yarn.

8: For Owl Bag, with black, whipstitch H and I pieces wrong sides together as indicated; overcast unfinished edges. Using 2" lengths, make six ½" [13mm] loops; glue loops to wrong side of Owl Motif (see photo) and glue Owl Motif to one side of Bag. Twist remaining lengths of yarn together for handle; glue to Bag as shown.

9: Cut Owl's Beak from orange felt or buckram according to Owl Beak Pattern; glue to Owl Motif. Glue two half round beads to Owl Motif; stuff tissue paper into Owl Bag and glue candies to tissue paper. Hang Owl Bag over one arm of Kitty; glue to secure.

A – Kitty Head Front
(13w x 13h-hole piece)
Cut 1 & work.

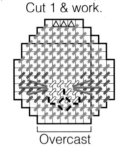

Overcast

A – Kitty Head Back
(13w x 13h-hole piece)
Cut 1 & work.

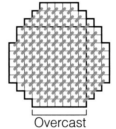

Overcast

C – Kitty Hand Front
(6w x 7h-hole pieces)
Cut 2 & work.

Overcast

C – Kitty Hand Back
(6w x 7h-hole pieces)
Cut 2 & work.

Overcast

B – Kitty Body Front
(18w x 21h-hole piece)
Cut 1 & work.

Overcast

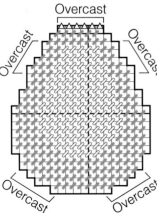

Overcast · Overcast · Overcast · Overcast

B – Kitty Body Back
(18w x 21h-hole piece)
Cut 1 & work.

Overcast

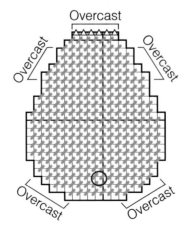

Overcast · Overcast · Overcast · Overcast

E – Kitty Tail Tip
(4w x 5h-hole pieces)
Cut 2 & work.

Overcast

D – Kitty Foot Top
(6w x 8h-hole pieces)
Cut 2 & work.

Overcast

D – Kitty Foot Bottom
(6w x 8h-hole pieces)
Cut 2 & work.

Overcast

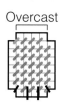

Kitty Ear Patterns
(actual sizes)

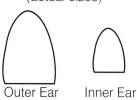

Outer Ear   Inner Ear

F – Pumpkin Front
(13w x 13h-hole piece)
Cut 1 & work.

Overcast

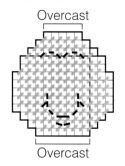

Overcast

F – Pumpkin Back
(13w x 13h-hole piece)
Cut 1 & work.

Overcast

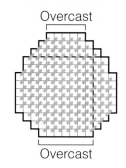

Overcast

Pumpkin Nose Pattern
(actual size)

Pumpkin Collar Pattern
(actual size)

G – Owl Motif
(13w x 12h-hole piece)
Cut 1 & work.

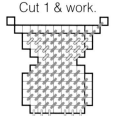

COLOR KEY
Trick or Treat Kitty

TWO STRANDS
EMBROIDERY FLOSS

Black
1 yd. [0.9m]

SIX STRANDS
EMBROIDERY FLOSS

Black
1 yd. [0.9m]

WORSTED-WEIGHT		NEED-LOFT®
Silver 25 yds. [22.9m]		#37
Black 10 yds. [9.1m]		#00
Orange 10 yds. [9.1m]		—
Pink 4 yds. [3.7m]		#07
White 4 yds. [3.7m]		#41
Yellow 1 yd. [0.9m]		#57

I – Owl Bag End
(5w x 28h-hole piece)
Cut 1 & work.

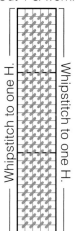

Whipstitch to one H.

Whipstitch to one H.

H – Owl Bag Side
(7w x 11h-hole pieces)
Cut 2 & work.

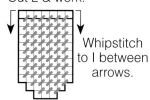

Whipstitch to I between arrows.

Owl Beak Pattern
(actual size)

STITCH KEY

⊟ Backstitch/Straight
● French Knot
▲ Modified Turkey Work

ATTACHMENT KEY

⊙ Tail

Skeleton

Designed by Phyllis Dobbs

Make no bones about it! This door hanger will greet your guests with a great big grin!

SIZE: 10¼" x 23" [26cm x 58.4cm]

SKILL LEVEL: Average

MATERIALS:
- One 13½" x 21½" [34.3cm x 57.2cm] sheet of 7-mesh plastic canvas
- Craft glue or glue gun
- Worsted-weight or plastic canvas yarn (for amounts see Color Key)

CUTTING INSTRUCTIONS:
A: For Skeleton, cut one according to graph.
B: For Hat, cut one according to graph.
C: For Pumpkin, cut one according to graph.

STITCHING INSTRUCTIONS:
1: Using colors indicated and continental stitch, work pieces according to graphs; with matching colors, overcast edges of pieces.

NOTE: Cut one 5" [12.7cm] length of fern.

2: For Pumpkin hanger, glue each end of yarn length to wrong side of C as shown in photo; glue center of hanger to wrong side of Skeleton's hand as shown.

3: Glue Hat to right side of Skeleton's head as shown; hang or display as desired.

C – Pumpkin
(22w x 18h-hole piece)
Cut 1 & work, leaving uncoded areas unworked.

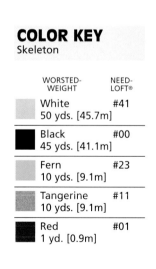

B – Hat
(32w x 22h-hole piece)
Cut 1 & work.

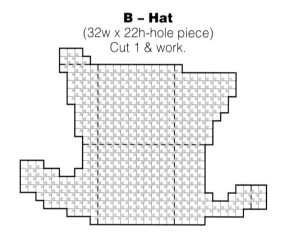

Pattern is divided onto two pages.

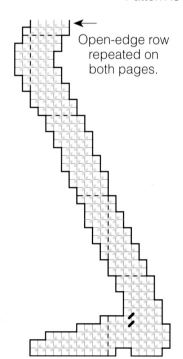

← Open-edge row repeated on both pages.

Open-edge row repeated on both pages. →

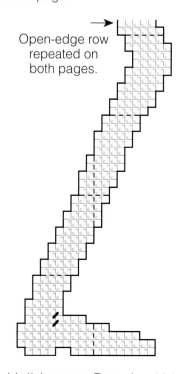

COLOR KEY
Skeleton

	WORSTED-WEIGHT	NEED-LOFT®
	White 50 yds. [45.7m]	#41
	Black 45 yds. [41.1m]	#00
	Fern 10 yds. [9.1m]	#23
	Tangerine 10 yds. [9.1m]	#11
	Red 1 yd. [0.9m]	#01

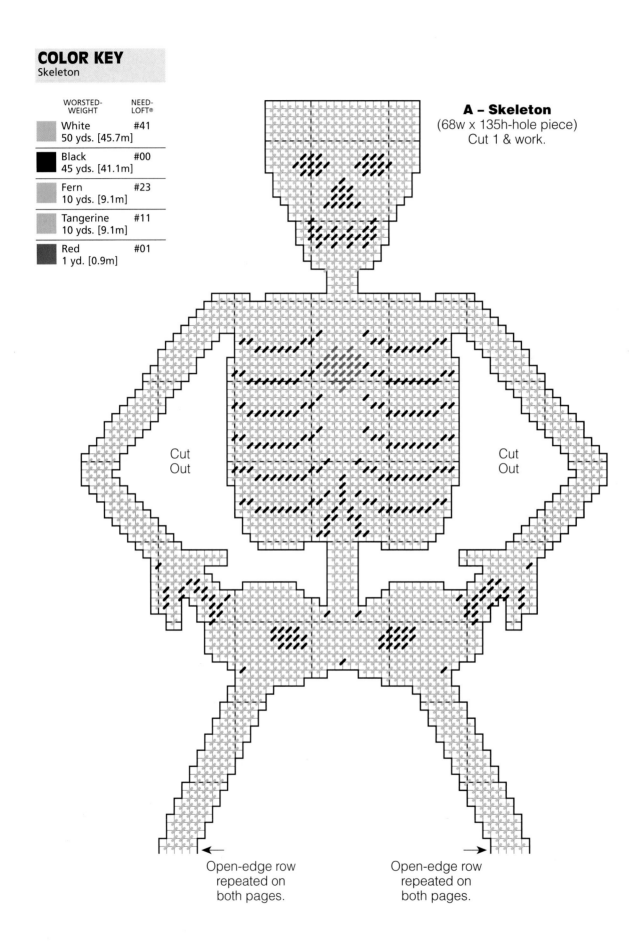

COLOR KEY
Skeleton

	WORSTED-WEIGHT	NEED-LOFT®
White	50 yds. [45.7m]	#41
Black	45 yds. [41.1m]	#00
Fern	10 yds. [9.1m]	#23
Tangerine	10 yds. [9.1m]	#11
Red	1 yd. [0.9m]	#01

A – Skeleton
(68w x 135h-hole piece)
Cut 1 & work.

Cut
Out

Cut
Out

← Open-edge row
repeated on
both pages.

Open-edge row →
repeated on
both pages.

Pumpkin Pin

Designed by Pam Bull

Accessorize throughout the fall with this smiling pumpkin pin.

SIZE: 1⅜" x 3" long [3.5cm x 7.6cm]

SKILL LEVEL: Average

MATERIALS:
- Scrap piece of each ivory and black 14-mesh plastic canvas
- One 1¼" [3.2cm] bar pin
- Craft glue or glue gun
- Six-strand embroidery floss (for amounts see Color Key)

CUTTING INSTRUCTIONS:
A: For Bar, cut one from black 19w x 5h-holes.
B: For Pumpkins #1 and #2, cut number indicated on graphs from ivory according to graphs.

STITCHING INSTRUCTIONS:
1: Using six strands floss in colors and stitches indicated, work pieces according to graphs; with dk. burnt orange for bar and with matching colors, overcast edges of pieces.

2: Cut one each 1" [2.5cm], 1¼" [3.2cm] and 2" [5.1cm] lengths of black; position and glue one end of each length to wrong side of Bar and remaining end of each length to wrong side of one Pumpkin as shown in photo.

3: Glue wrong side of Bar to bar pin.

A – Bar
(19w x 5h-hole piece)
Cut 1 from black & work.

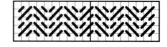

B – Pumpkin #1
(16w x 18h-hole pieces)
Cut 2 from ivory & work.

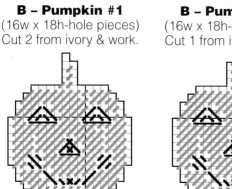

B – Pumpkin #2
(16w x 18h-hole pieces)
Cut 1 from ivory & work.

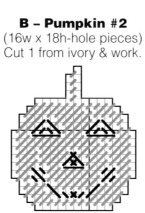

COLOR KEY
Pumpkin Pin

	EMBROIDERY FLOSS	DMC®
	Dk. Burnt Orange 20 yds. [18.3m]	#900
	Black 8 yds. [7.3m]	#310
	Dk. Pistachio Green 2 yds. [1.8m]	#367

Thanksgiving!

Plan on leaving the kitchen early this holiday season. Receive bountiful blessings of peace and relaxation as you stitch away the hours.

Tom Turkey

Designed by Lee Lindeman

This turkey will not stick his neck out this Thanksgiving!

SIZE: 5" x 10¾" x 9" tall [12.7cm x 27.3cm x 22.9], when sitting

SKILL LEVEL: Challenging

MATERIALS:
- Three sheets of 7-mesh plastic canvas
- Two 10mm glass eyes
- Scrap piece of black buckram or plastic foam sheet
- One ½" [13mm] dowel rod
- 10 yd. [9.1m] spool of black 18-gauge wire
- Polyester fiberfill
- Craft glue or glue gun
- Worsted-weight or plastic canvas yarn (for amounts see Color Key)

CUTTING INSTRUCTIONS:
A: For Head Front and Back, cut two (one for Front and one for Back) according to graph.
B: For Neck, cut two according to graph.
C: For Body Front and Back, cut two (one for Front and one for Back) according to graph.
D: For Bottom, cut one according to graph.
E: For Wings #1 and #2, cut two each according to graphs.
F: For Tail, cut two according to graph.
G: For Feet, cut four according to graph.

STITCHING INSTRUCTIONS:
1: Using colors and stitches indicated, work pieces according to graphs; with matching colors, overcast indicated edges of A, B and G pieces.

2: Using black (Separate into individual plies, if desired.) and French knot, embroider freckles on Front A as indicated on graph.

3: For Head, with red, whipstitch A pieces wrong sides together, stuffing face lightly with fiberfill before closing. Using red and modified turkey work (Leave 1" [2.5cm] loops.), embroider crown as indicated. Cut through loops; fray and trim ends as desired.

4: With red, whipstitch B pieces wrong sides together as indicated. Insert Head in opening of Neck as shown in photo; glue to secure.

NOTE: For each Leg (make 2), tightly coil wire around dowel rod until leg is approximately 2½" [6.4cm] in length.

5: With brown, whipstitch C and D pieces wrong sides together as indicated, stuffing Body generously with fiberfill before closing. Twist and screw legs into place as indicated on one C for Front.

6: For each Foot (make 2), with black, whipstitch two G pieces wrong sides together, securing over end of one leg before closing.

7: For each Wing (make 2), with matching colors, whipstitch one E#1 and one E#2 wrong sides together. Glue to Body Front as shown.

8: For Tail, with matching colors, whipstitch F pieces wrong sides together; matching bottom edges, glue to Body Back as shown.

NOTES: Cut beak pieces from buckram or plastic foam.
Cut two 3½" [8.9cm] strands of red.

9: Glue Neck to Body Front (see photo). Glue eyes and beaks to Head Front. For wattle, twist strands of yarn together; glue to one side of Beak as shown in photo.

Beak Patterns
(actual sizes)

Upper Beak

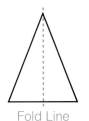

Fold Line

Lower Beak

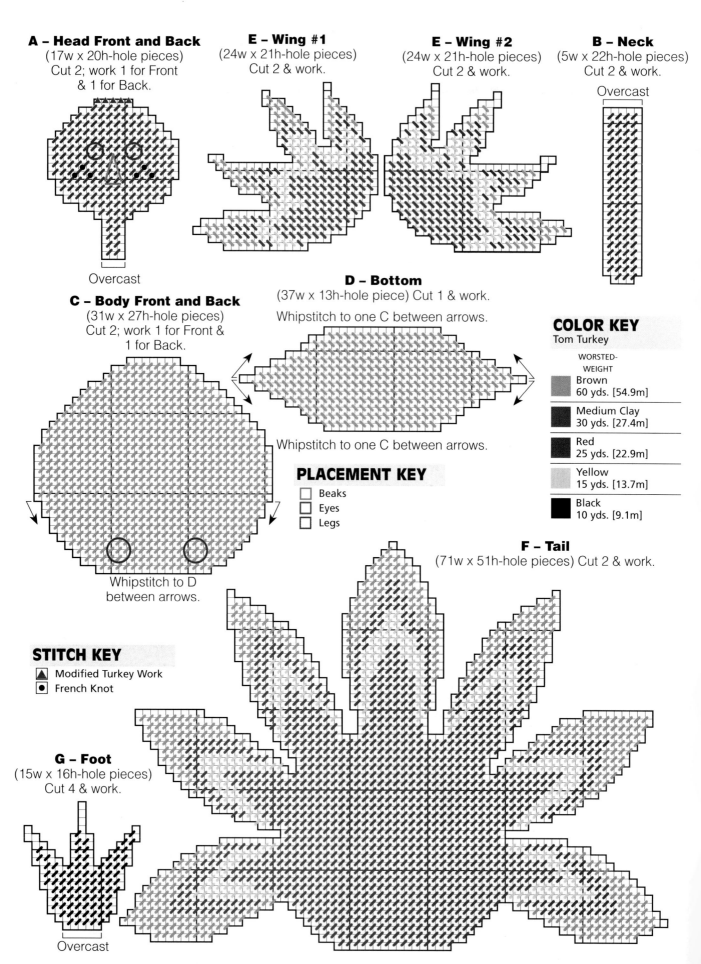

A – Head Front and Back
(17w x 20h-hole pieces)
Cut 2; work 1 for Front
& 1 for Back.

Overcast

E – Wing #1
(24w x 21h-hole pieces)
Cut 2 & work.

E – Wing #2
(24w x 21h-hole pieces)
Cut 2 & work.

B – Neck
(5w x 22h-hole pieces)
Cut 2 & work.

Overcast

C – Body Front and Back
(31w x 27h-hole pieces)
Cut 2; work 1 for Front &
1 for Back.

Whipstitch to D
between arrows.

D – Bottom
(37w x 13h-hole piece) Cut 1 & work.

Whipstitch to one C between arrows.

Whipstitch to one C between arrows.

PLACEMENT KEY
- Beaks
- Eyes
- Legs

COLOR KEY
Tom Turkey

WORSTED-
WEIGHT
- Brown
  60 yds. [54.9m]
- Medium Clay
  30 yds. [27.4m]
- Red
  25 yds. [22.9m]
- Yellow
  15 yds. [13.7m]
- Black
  10 yds. [9.1m]

F – Tail
(71w x 51h-hole pieces) Cut 2 & work.

STITCH KEY
- ▲ Modified Turkey Work
- ● French Knot

G – Foot
(15w x 16h-hole pieces)
Cut 4 & work.

Overcast

Give Thanks

Designed by Angie Arickx

This friendly scarecrow reminds one and all to give thanks this season.

SIZE: 8¾" x 11⅛" [22.2cm x 28.3cm]

SKILL LEVEL: Easy

MATERIALS:
• One sheet of 7-mesh plastic canvas
• Worsted-weight or plastic canvas yarn
  (for amounts see Color Key)

CUTTING INSTRUCTIONS:
For Give Thanks, cut one according to graph.

STITCHING INSTRUCTIONS:
1: Using colors and stitches indicated, work piece according to graph; with matching colors, overcast edges of piece.

2: Hang as desired.

Give Thanks
(74w x 58h-hole piece)
Cut 1 & work.

COLOR KEY
Give Thanks

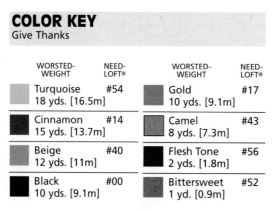

	WORSTED-WEIGHT	NEED-LOFT®		WORSTED-WEIGHT	NEED-LOFT®
	Turquoise 18 yds. [16.5m]	#54		Gold 10 yds. [9.1m]	#17
	Cinnamon 15 yds. [13.7m]	#14		Camel 8 yds. [7.3m]	#43
	Beige 12 yds. [11m]	#40		Flesh Tone 2 yds. [1.8m]	#56
	Black 10 yds. [9.1m]	#00		Bittersweet 1 yd. [0.9m]	#52

Turkeys

Designed by Kristine Loffredo

Invite these turkeys to join your family's holiday feast.

SIZES: Treat Box is 4" x 10" x 12" tall [10.2cm x 25.4cm x 30.5cm]; Wall Hanging is 15" x 22½" [38.1cm x 57.2cm]

SKILL LEVEL: Average

MATERIALS:
• One 13½" x 22½" [34.3cm x 57.2cm] and two standard-size sheets of 7-mesh plastic canvas
• Two 12mm and two 20mm oval wiggle eyes
• 15" x 22½" [38.1cm x 57.2cm] sheet of ¼"- thick [6mm] cardboard
• Craft glue or glue gun
• Metallic craft cord (for amount see Color Key)
• Worsted-weight or plastic canvas yarn (for amounts see Color Key

CUTTING INSTRUCTIONS:
A: For Treat Holder Back, cut one from standard-size sheet according to graph.
B: For Treat Holder Beak, cut one from standard-size sheet according to graph.
C: For Treat Holder Sides, cut two from standard-size sheet 25w x 14h-holes (no graph).
D: For Treat Holder Front, cut one from standard-size sheet 41w x 14h-holes (no graph).
E: For Treat Holder Bottom, cut one from standard-size sheet 41w x 25h-holes (no graph).
F: For Turkey, cut one from large sheet according to graph.
G: For Turkey Beak, cut one from standard-size sheet according to graph.
H: For Turkey Wings #1 and #2, cut one each from standard-size sheet according to graphs.
I: For Turkey Backing, using F as a pattern, cut one from cardboard ⅛" [3mm] smaller at all edges.

STITCHING INSTRUCTIONS:
NOTE: E is not worked.

1: Leaving attachment areas unworked, using colors and stitches indicated, work A, B and F-H pieces according to graphs; work C and D pieces according to Treat Holder Front and Side Stitch Pattern Guide. Omitting attachment areas, with matching colors, overcast edges of A, B and F-H pieces.

2: Using cord and embroidery stitches indicated, embroider detail on A and F pieces as indicated on graphs.

3: With lemon, whipstitch B to right side of A and G to right side of F as indicated.

4: For Holder, whipstitch A and C-E pieces together according to Treat Holder Assembly Illustration on page __; using cord, overcast unfinished edges of Holder. Glue 12mm wiggle eyes to turkey (see photo).

5: Glue 20mm wiggle eyes to right side of F (see photo); glue wrong side of each H to right side of F as indicated and Backing to wrong side of F. Hang as desired.

B – Treat Holder Beak
(9w x 13h-hole piece)
Cut 1 from standard
sheet & work.

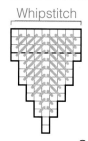

G – Turkey Beak
(11w x 18h-hole piece)
Cut 1 from standard sheet & work.

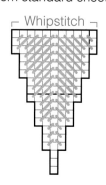

Treat Holder Assembly Illustration
(Pieces are shown in different colors for contrast; gray denotes wrong side.)

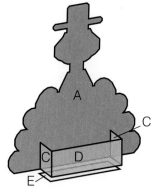

COLOR KEY
Turkeys

CRAFT CORD		NEED-LOFT®
	Gold 5 yds. [4.6m]	#01

WORSTED-WEIGHT		NEED-LOFT®
	Cinnamon 60 yds. [54.9m]	#14
	Forest 30 yds. [27.4m]	#29
	Holly 30 yds. [27.4m]	#27
	Camel 25 yds. [22.9m]	#43
	Red 20 yds. [18.3m]	#01
	Bt. Blue 15 yds. [13.7m]	#60
	Pumpkin 10 yds. [9.1m]	#12
	Yellow 8 yds. [7.3m]	#57
	Maple 5 yds. [4.6m]	#13
	Gold 4 yds. [3.7m]	#17
	Lemon 4 yds. [3.7m]	#20
	Bittersweet 3 yds. [2.7m]	#52
	Black 3 yds. [2.7m]	#00

ATTACHMENT KEY

☐ Beak/Turkey
☐ Side/Back
☐ Wing/Turkey

H – Turkey Wing #2
(26w x 53h-hole piece)
Cut 1 from standard sheet & work.

H – Turkey Wing #1
(26w x 53h-hole piece)
Cut 1 from standard sheet & work.

A – Treat Holder Back
(67w x 79h-hole piece)
Cut 1 from standard sheet & work.

STITCH KEY

⊟ Backstitch/Straight

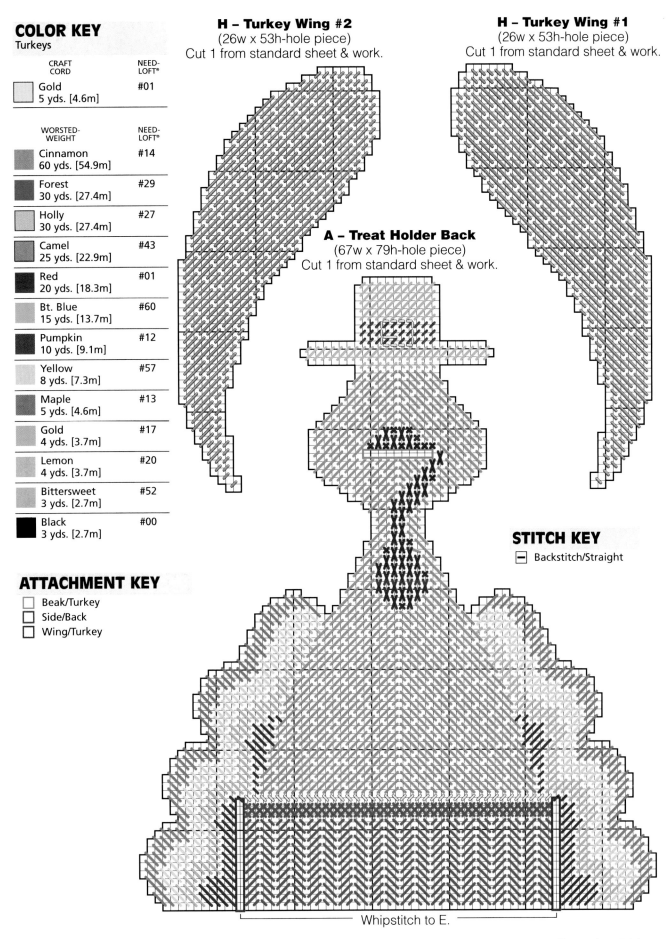

Whipstitch to E.

COLOR KEY
Turkeys

	CRAFT CORD	NEED-LOFT®
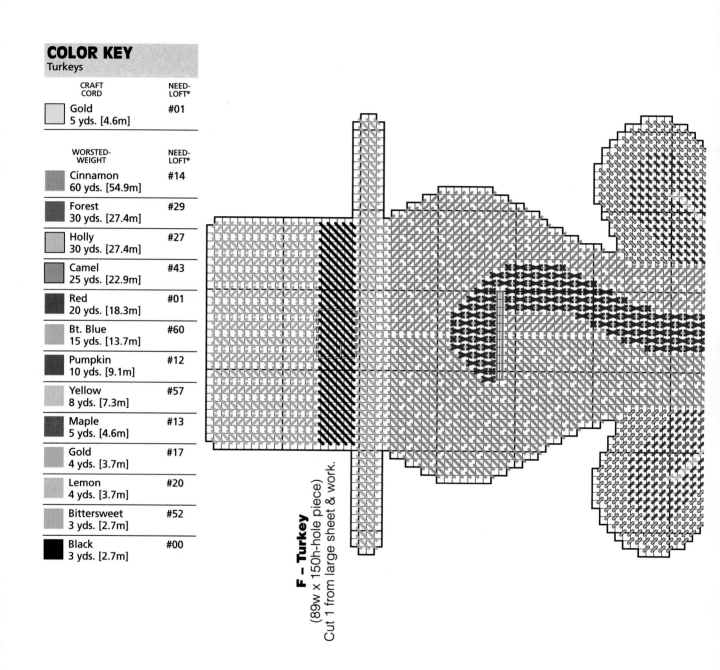 Gold 5 yds. [4.6m]		#01

	WORSTED-WEIGHT	NEED-LOFT®
Cinnamon 60 yds. [54.9m]		#14
Forest 30 yds. [27.4m]		#29
Holly 30 yds. [27.4m]		#27
Camel 25 yds. [22.9m]		#43
Red 20 yds. [18.3m]		#01
Bt. Blue 15 yds. [13.7m]		#60
Pumpkin 10 yds. [9.1m]		#12
Yellow 8 yds. [7.3m]		#57
Maple 5 yds. [4.6m]		#13
Gold 4 yds. [3.7m]		#17
Lemon 4 yds. [3.7m]		#20
Bittersweet 3 yds. [2.7m]		#52
Black 3 yds. [2.7m]		#00

F – Turkey
(89w x 150h-hole piece)
Cut 1 from large sheet & work.

ATTACHMENT KEY
 Beak/Turkey
Side/Back
Wing/Turkey

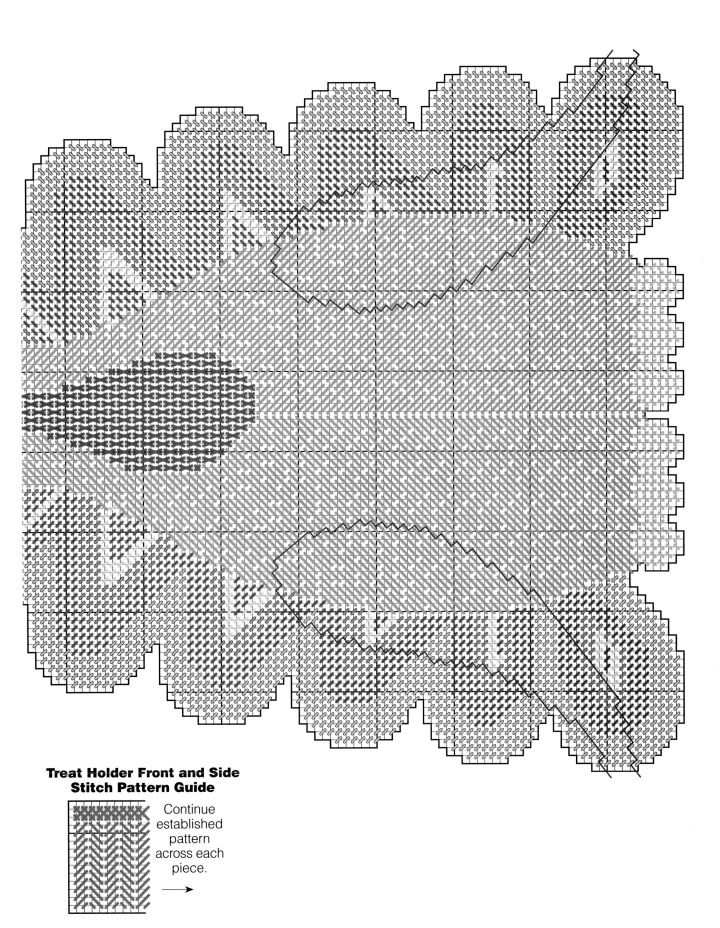

**Treat Holder Front and Side
Stitch Pattern Guide**

Continue
established
pattern
across each
piece.

Share The Harvest

Designed by by Kathleen Hurley

Pilgrims remind us to share our blessings of abundance.

SIZE: 11¾" x 17¼" [29.8cm x 43.8cm]

SKILL LEVEL: Average

MATERIALS:
- 2½ sheets of 7-mesh plastic canvas
- Worsted-weight or plastic canvas yarn
  (for amounts see Color Key)

CUTTING INSTRUCTIONS:
A: For Pilgrim Girl, cut one according to graph.
B: For Pilgrim Boy, cut one according to graph.
C: For Wreath, cut one according to graph.
D: For Sign, cut one 64w x 42h-holes.
E: For Pumpkins #1 and #2, cut number indicated according to graphs.
F: For Flowers, cut ten according to graph.
G: For Leaves, cut ten according to graph.

STITCHING INSTRUCTIONS:
1: Using colors and stitches indicated, work pieces according to graphs; with pumpkin for

Sign and Pumpkins and with matching colors as shown in photo, overcast edges of pieces.

2: Using colors (Separate into individual plies, if desired.) and embroidery stitches indicated, embroider detail on A, B and D pieces as indicated on graphs.

3: Glue Girl, Boy, three Pumpkins and six each Flower and Leaves to Wreath as shown or as desired. Glue remaining Pumpkins, Leaves and Flowers to Sign as shown or as desired.

4: Cut two 3" [7.6cm] lengths of black; glue one end of each length to wrong side of D and remaining end of each length to wrong side of C (see photo). Hang as desired.

STITCH KEY
- − Backstitch/Straight
- ● French Knot

F – Flower
(6w x 6h-hole pieces)
Cut 10 & work.

G – Leaf
(3w x 8h-hole pieces)
Cut 10 & work.

E – Pumpkin #1
(18w x 18h-hole pieces)
Cut 4 & work.

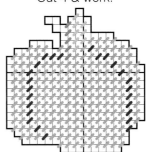

E – Pumpkin #2
(18w x 18h-hole pieces)
Cut 2 & work.

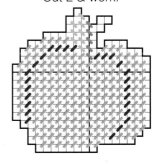

COLOR KEY
Share The Harvest

	WORSTED-WEIGHT	NEED-LOFT®		WORSTED-WEIGHT	NEED-LOFT®
	White 50 yds. [45.7m]	#41		Yellow 10 yds. [9.1m]	#57
	Fern 40 yds. [36.6m]	#23		Bright Blue 7 yds. [6.4m]	#60
	Tangerine 30 yds. [27.4m]	#11		Black 6 yds. [5.5m]	#00
	Camel 15 yds. [13.7m]	#43		Flesh Tone 5 yds. [4.6m]	#56
	Pumpkin 15 yds. [13.7m]	#12		Red 4 yds. [3.7m]	#01
	Holly 12 yds. [11m]	#27		Gold 3 yds. [2.7m]	#17
	Gray 10 yds. [9.1m]	#38		Pink 1 yd. [0.9m]	#07
	Royal 10 yds. [9.1m]	#32			

A – Pilgrim Girl
(51w x 51h-hole piece)
Cut 1 & work.

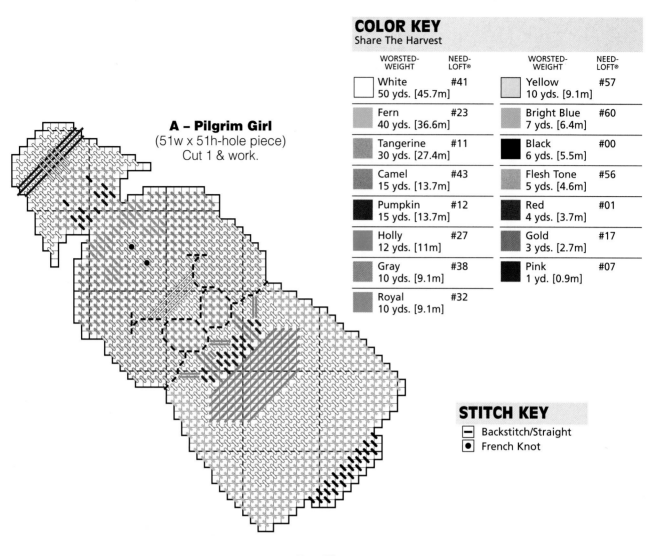

COLOR KEY
Share The Harvest

	WORSTED-WEIGHT	NEED-LOFT®		WORSTED-WEIGHT	NEED-LOFT®
	White 50 yds. [45.7m]	#41		Yellow 10 yds. [9.1m]	#57
	Fern 40 yds. [36.6m]	#23		Bright Blue 7 yds. [6.4m]	#60
	Tangerine 30 yds. [27.4m]	#11		Black 6 yds. [5.5m]	#00
	Camel 15 yds. [13.7m]	#43		Flesh Tone 5 yds. [4.6m]	#56
	Pumpkin 15 yds. [13.7m]	#12		Red 4 yds. [3.7m]	#01
	Holly 12 yds. [11m]	#27		Gold 3 yds. [2.7m]	#17
	Gray 10 yds. [9.1m]	#38		Pink 1 yd. [0.9m]	#07
	Royal 10 yds. [9.1m]	#32			

STITCH KEY
- — Backstitch/Straight
- ● French Knot

D – Sign
(64w x 42h-hole piece) Cut 1 & work.

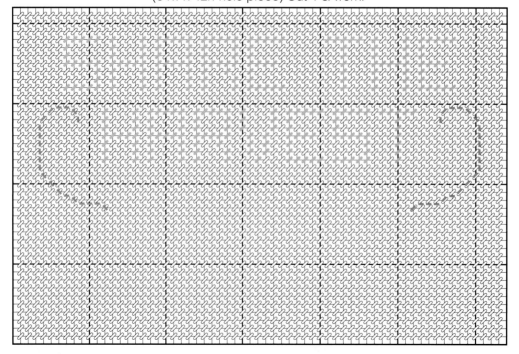

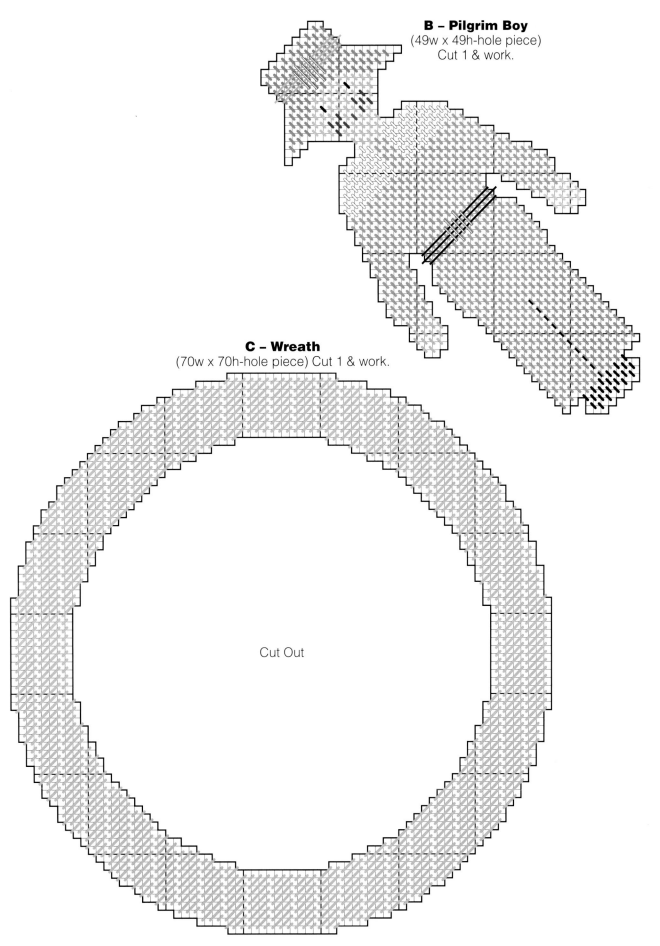

B – Pilgrim Boy
(49w x 49h-hole piece)
Cut 1 & work.

C – Wreath
(70w x 70h-hole piece) Cut 1 & work.

Cut Out

Happy Hanukkah!

*T*he celebration of this eight day Jewish
holiday brings family and friends together
for worship and reflection of past and present.

Menorah With Frame

Designed by Mary Perry

Display your favorite Hanukkah memories in a frame with the Menorah.

SIZE: 3" x 7" x 6" tall [7.6cm x 17.8cm x 15.2cm] with a 3⅝" x 4¾" [9.2cm x 12.1cm] photo window.

SKILL LEVEL: Average

MATERIALS:
- 1½ sheets of 7-mesh plastic canvas
- ³⁄₁₆" [5mm] metallic ribbon (for amount see Color Key)
- Worsted-weight or plastic canvas yarn (for amounts see Color Key)

CUTTING INSTRUCTIONS:
A: For Motif Front, cut one 47w x 39h-holes.
B: For Frame Front, cut one according to graph.
C: For Frame Backing, cut one according to graph.
D: For Frame Supports, cut two according to graph.

STITCHING INSTRUCTIONS:
NOTE: C is not worked.

1: Using colors indicated and continental stitch, work A, B and D pieces according to graphs; with dk. blue, overcast cutout edges of B.

2: Using metallic ribbon and yarn in colors and straight stitch, embroider detail on A as indicated on graph.

3: For Frame, with dk. blue, whipstitch C to wrong side of B at side and bottom edges as indicated on graph; whipstitch top edge of Frame to A as indicated through all thicknesses.

4: With dk. blue, whipstitch D pieces to A; overcast all unfinished edges. Each Frame Support fits into one slot on Frame.

A – Motif Front
(47w x 39h-hole piece) Cut 1 & work.

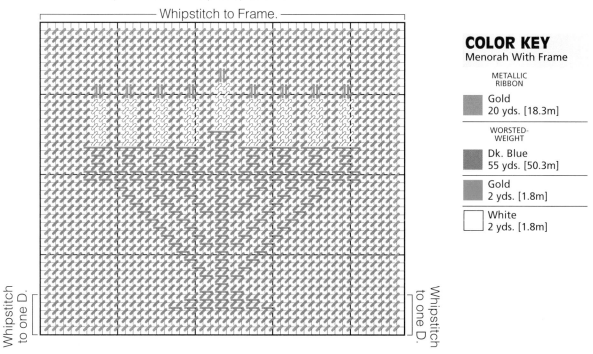

COLOR KEY
Menorah With Frame

METALLIC RIBBON		
■	Gold	20 yds. [18.3m]

WORSTED-WEIGHT		
■	Dk. Blue	55 yds. [50.3m]
■	Gold	2 yds. [1.8m]
□	White	2 yds. [1.8m]

C – Frame Backing
(47w x 39h-hole piece) Cut 1 & work.

Whipstitch to A & B.

Whipstitch to B between arrows.

Whipstitch to B between arrows.

COLOR KEY
Menorah With Frame

METALLIC RIBBON

Gold
20 yds. [18.3m]

WORSTED-WEIGHT

Dk. Blue
55 yds. [50.3m]

Gold
2 yds. [1.8m]

White
2 yds. [1.8m]

STITCH KEY

– Straight

D – Frame Support
(20w x 5h-hole pieces)
Cut 2. Work 1 & 1 reversed.

Whipstitch to A.

B – Frame Front
(47w x 39h-hole piece) Cut 1 & work.

Whipstitch to A & C.

Whipstitch to C between arrows.

Cut Out

Whipstitch to C between arrows.

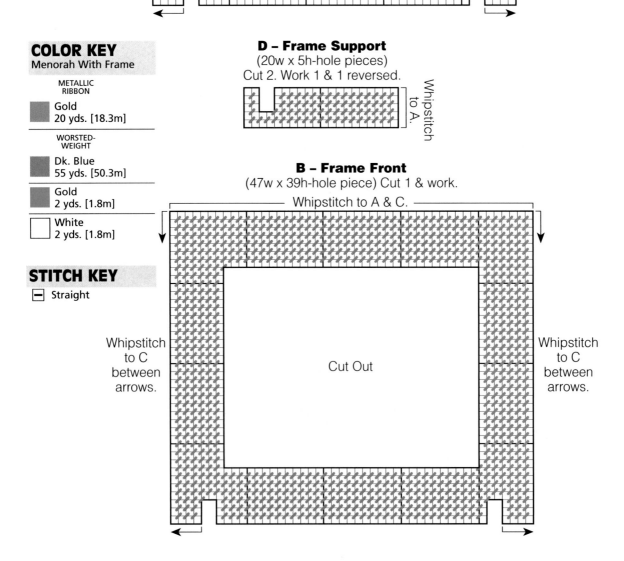

Merry Christmas!

Create visions of sugarplums throughout the house by stitching these festive projects for your holiday décor.

Plaid Bears

Designed by Janelle Giese of Janelle Marie Designs

Let these busy plaid bears help decorate your home this holiday.

SIZES: Card Holder is 2¾" x 10½" x 18¼" tall [7cm x 26.7cm x 46.4cm]; Candle Holder is 5½" x 8¾" x 6¾" tall [14cm x 22.2cm x 17.1cm]; each Coaster is 3½" x 3½" [8.9cm x 8.9cm]; Coaster Holder is 3⅞" x 1⅜" x 3⅞" [9.8cm x 3.5cm x 9.8cm]; Tissue Cover loosely covers a boutique-style tissue box; Tree Ornament is 2⅜" x 3" [6cm x 7.6cm], not including hanger

SKILL LEVEL: Challenging

MATERIALS:
- Ten sheets of 7-mesh plastic canvas
- Two cups of gravel or other weighting material
- Velcro® closure (optional)
- Craft glue or glue gun
- No. 5 pearl cotton (for amount see Color Key)

- #32 heavy metallic braid (for amounts see Color Key)
- Chenille yarn or worsted-weight (for amounts see Color Key), Worsted-weight or plastic canvas yarn (for amounts see Color Key)

CUTTING INSTRUCTIONS:
A: For Card Holder Back Pieces #1 and #2, cut one each according to graphs.
B: For Card Holder Ends #1 and #2, cut one each according to graphs.
C: For Card Holder Front, cut one 57w x 33h-holes.
D: For Card Holder Bottom, cut one 57w x 17h-holes (no graph).
E: For Candle Holder Motif, cut one according to graph.

F: For Candle Holder Center Column Outer Pieces, cut four according to graph.
G: For Candle Holder Center Column Inner Piece, cut four 21w x 34h-holes.
H: For Candle Holder Sides, cut eight 35w x 11h-holes
I: For Candle Holder Side Supports, cut three according to graph.
J: For Candle Holder Inner Base Pieces, cut two 21w x 21h-holes (no graph).
K: For Candle Holder Bottom, cut one 35w x 35h-holes.
L: For Tree Motifs, cut six according to graph.
M: For Coasters, cut four according to graph.
N: For Coaster Holder Sides, cut two according to graph.
O: For Coaster Holder Ends and Bottom, cut three (two for Ends and one for Bottom) 8w x 25h-holes (no graph).
P: For Tissue Cover Top, cut one according to graph.
Q: For Tissue Cover Sides, cut four 31w x 39h-holes.
R: For Tissue Cover Optional Bottom and Flap, cut one 31w x 31h-holes for Bottom and one 31w x 12h-holes for Flap (no graphs).

STITCHING INSTRUCTIONS:
NOTE: J, K and R pieces are not worked.

1: Using colors and stitches indicated, work A - C, E-I, L-N, P and Q pieces according to graphs. Using forest and continental stitch, work D and O pieces.

2: With black for Coasters and with matching colors as shown in photo, overcast edges of E, L and M pieces and cutout edges of P.

3: Using pearl cotton or six strands floss and braid in colors and embroidery stitches indicated, embroider detail on A-C, E, F, H, L, N, P and Q pieces as indicated on graphs.

4: Omitting attachment areas, with matching colors as shown and as indicated on graphs, whipstitch cutouts and outer edges of A pieces together. With black, whipstitch A-D pieces together as indicated, forming Card Holder; overcast unfinished edges.

5: For Candle Holder, whipstitch F-K pieces together according to Candle Holder Assembly Diagram on page 129. Glue wrong side of Candle Holder Motif to one side of Candle Holder as shown.

6: With black, whipstitch N and O pieces wrong sides together, forming Coaster Holder; overcast unfinished edges. Glue one Tree Motif to one Holder Side as shown.

7: With black, whipstitch P and Q pieces wrong sides together, forming Tissue Cover. For Optional Bottom, whipstitch R pieces together and to one Cover Side according to Optional Tissue Cover Bottom Illustration on page 129; glue closure to flap and inside Cover (see illustration). Overcast unfinished edges of Cover. Glue one Tree Motif to each Cover Side as shown.

8: For Tree Ornament, cut a 6" [15.2cm] length of braid; glue ends to wrong side of remaining Tree Motif.

STITCH KEY
- ⊟ Backstitch/Straight
- ● French Knot
- ◩ Lazy Daisy

COLOR KEY
Plaid Bears

NO. 5 PEARL COTTON		DMC®
■	Black 75 yds. [68.6m]	#310

METALLIC BRAID		KREINIK
▨	Gold 90 yds. [82.3m]	#002
▨	Silver 10 yds. [9.1m]	#001

CHENILLE YARN OR WORSTED-WEIGHT		HONEY SUCKLE
▨	Ivory 2½ oz. [70.9g]	#003
□	White 20 yds. [18.3m]	#001

WORSTED-WEIGHT		NEED-LOFT®
▨	Eggshell 4 oz. [113.4g]	#39
▨	Forest 2½ oz. [70.9g]	#29
▨	Red 2½ oz. [70.9g]	#01
▨	Black 60 yds. [54.9m]	#00
▨	Burgundy 60 yds. [54.9m]	#03
▨	Christmas Green 35 yds. [32m]	#28
▨	Royal 4 yds. [3.7m]	#32
▨	Dk. Royal 2 yds. [1.8m]	#48

A – Card Holder Back Piece #1
(69w x 90h-hole piece)
Cut 1. Position over A#2 at matching edges & work through both thicknesses as one.

Carefully cut out gray areas.

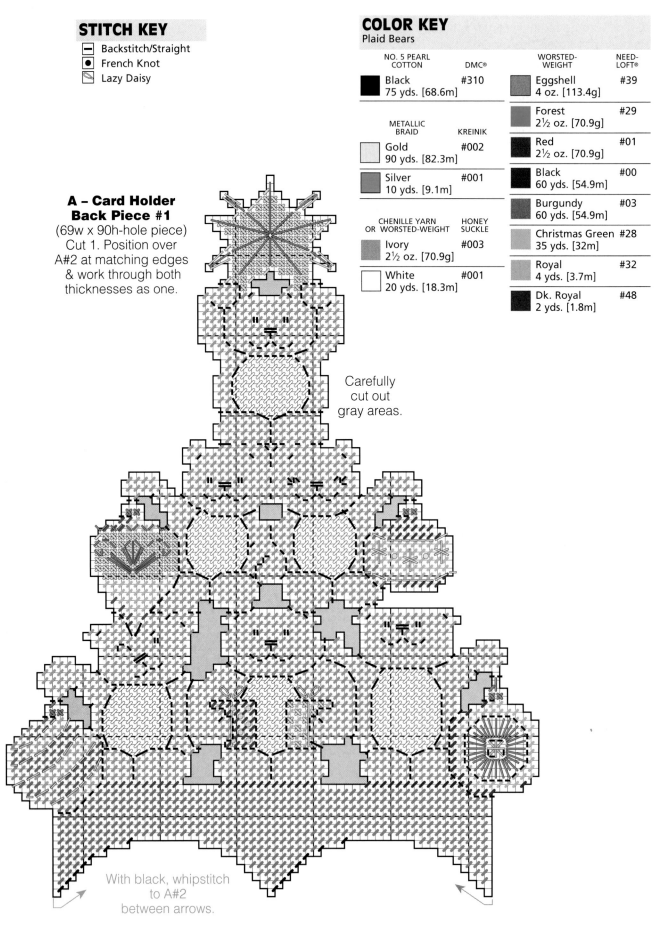

With black, whipstitch to A#2 between arrows.

A – Card Holder
Back Piece #2
(69w x 90h-hole piece)
Cut 1 & work, leaving
uncoded area unworked.

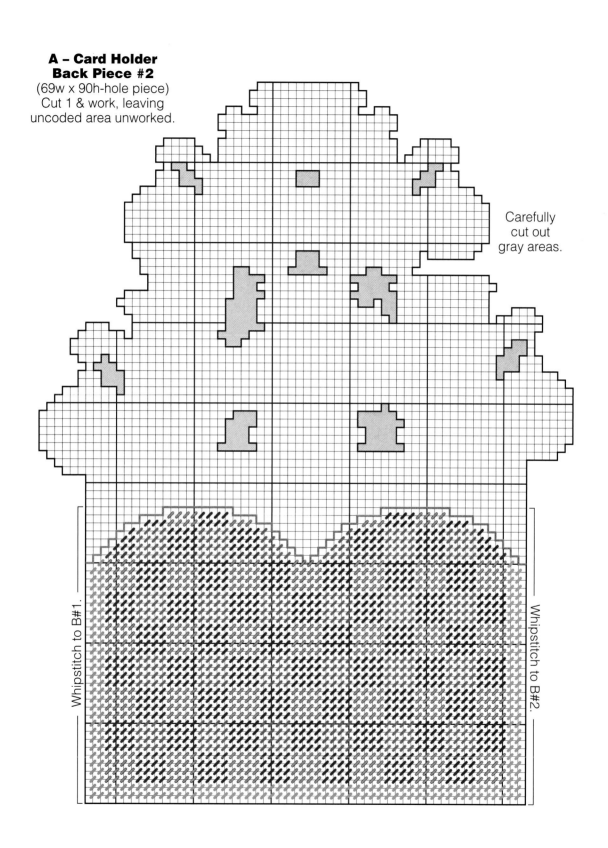

Carefully
cut out
gray areas.

Whipstitch to B#1.

Whipstitch to B#2.

COLOR KEY
Plaid Bears

	NO. 5 PEARL COTTON	DMC®		WORSTED-WEIGHT	NEED-LOFT®
■	Black 75 yds. [68.6m]	#310	▨	Eggshell 4 oz. [113.4g]	#39
	METALLIC BRAID	KREINIK	▨	Forest 2½ oz. [70.9g]	#29
▨	Gold 90 yds. [82.3m]	#002	■	Red 2½ oz. [70.9g]	#01
▨	Silver 10 yds. [9.1m]	#001	■	Black 60 yds. [54.9m]	#00
	CHENILLE YARN OR WORSTED-WEIGHT	HONEY SUCKLE	▨	Burgundy 60 yds. [54.9m]	#03
▨	Ivory 2½ oz. [70.9g]	#003	▨	Christmas Green 35 yds. [32m]	#28
□	White 20 yds. [18.3m]	#001	▨	Royal 4 yds. [3.7m]	#32
			▨	Dk. Royal 2 yds. [1.8m]	#48

STITCH KEY
- ⊟ Backstitch/Straight
- ⊡ French Knot
- ⊠ Lazy Daisy

G – Candle Holder Center Column Inner Piece
(21w x 34h-hole pieces)
Cut 4 & work, leaving
uncoded area unworked.

E – Candle Holder Motif
(57w x 44h-hole piece)
Cut 1 & work.

Carefully cut out gray areas.

F – Candle Holder Center Column Outer Piece
(21w x 42h-hole pieces)
Cut 4 & work, leaving uncoded areas unworked.

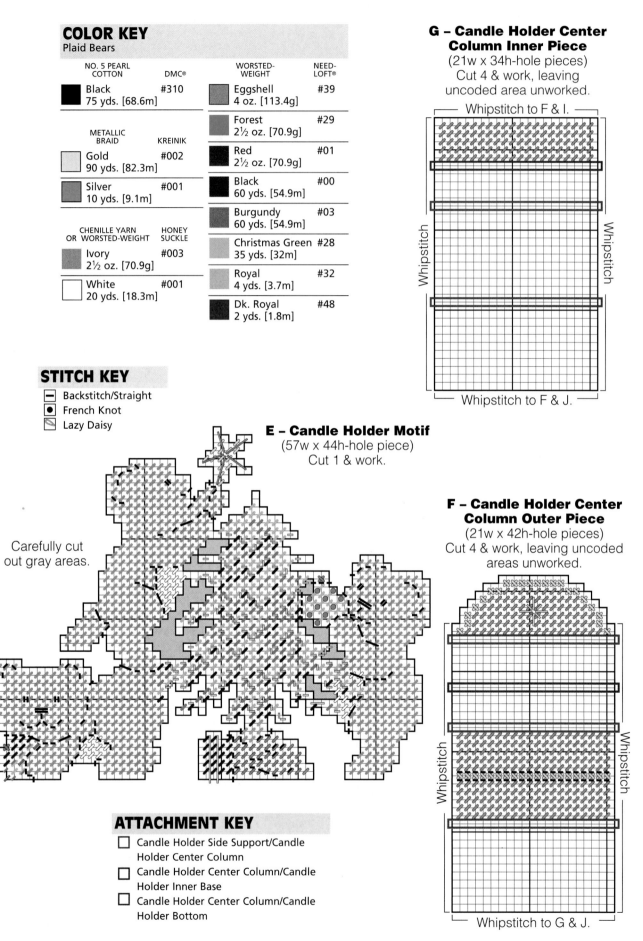

ATTACHMENT KEY
- □ Candle Holder Side Support/Candle Holder Center Column
- □ Candle Holder Center Column/Candle Holder Inner Base
- □ Candle Holder Center Column/Candle Holder Bottom

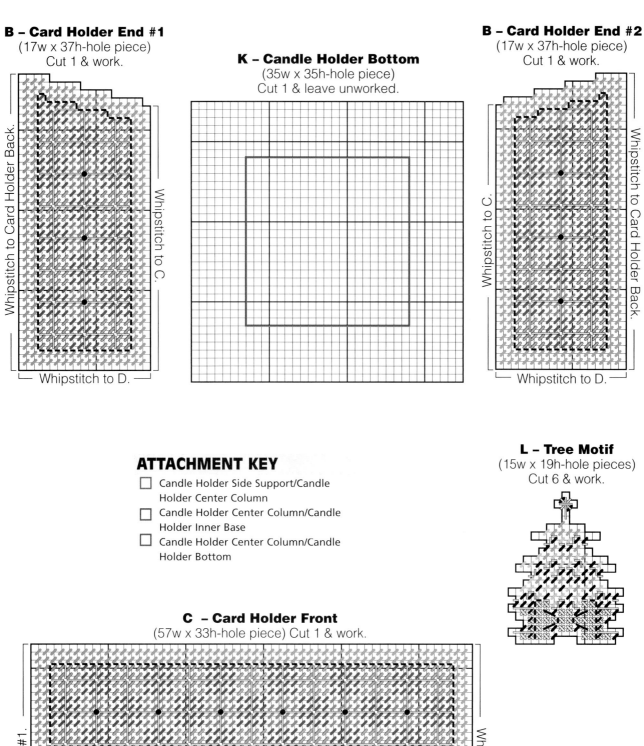

B – Card Holder End #1
(17w x 37h-hole piece)
Cut 1 & work.

Whipstitch to Card Holder Back.

Whipstitch to C.

Whipstitch to D.

K – Candle Holder Bottom
(35w x 35h-hole piece)
Cut 1 & leave unworked.

B – Card Holder End #2
(17w x 37h-hole piece)
Cut 1 & work.

Whipstitch to C.

Whipstitch to Card Holder Back.

Whipstitch to D.

ATTACHMENT KEY
☐ Candle Holder Side Support/Candle
   Holder Center Column
☐ Candle Holder Center Column/Candle
   Holder Inner Base
☐ Candle Holder Center Column/Candle
   Holder Bottom

L – Tree Motif
(15w x 19h-hole pieces)
Cut 6 & work.

C – Card Holder Front
(57w x 33h-hole piece) Cut 1 & work.

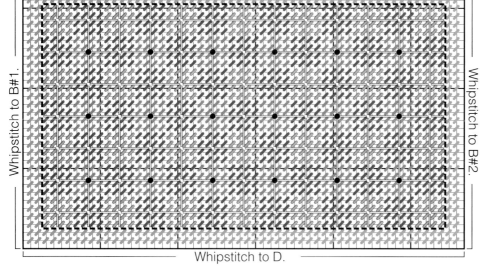

Whipstitch to B#1.

Whipstitch to B#2.

Whipstitch to D.

STITCH KEY
⊟ Backstitch/Straight
⦿ French Knot
◩ Lazy Daisy

H – Candle Holder Side
(35w x 11h-hole pieces) Cut 8 & work.

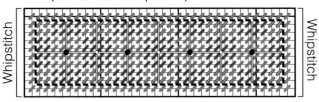

Whipstitch — Whipstitch

Q – Tissue Cover Side
(31w x 39h-hole pieces) Cut 4 & work.

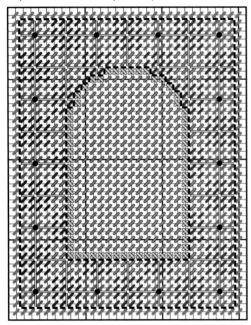

P – Tissue Cover Top
(31w x 31h-hole piece) Cut 1 & work.

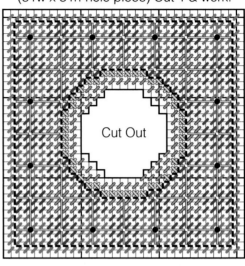

Cut Out

COLOR KEY
Plaid Bears

	NO. 5 PEARL COTTON	DMC®
■	Black 75 yds. [68.6m]	#310

	METALLIC BRAID	KREINIK
■	Gold 90 yds. [82.3m]	#002
■	Silver 10 yds. [9.1m]	#001

	CHENILLE YARN OR WORSTED-WEIGHT	HONEYSUCKLE
■	Ivory 2½ oz. [70.9g]	#003
□	White 20 yds. [18.3m]	#001

	WORSTED-WEIGHT	NEED-LOFT®
■	Eggshell 4 oz. [113.4g]	#39
■	Forest 2½ oz. [70.9g]	#29
■	Red 2½ oz. [70.9g]	#01
■	Black 60 yds. [54.9m]	#00
■	Burgundy 60 yds. [54.9m]	#03
■	Christmas Green 35 yds. [32m]	#28
■	Royal 4 yds. [3.7m]	#32
■	Dk. Royal 2 yds. [1.8m]	#48

N – Coaster Holder Side
(25w x 25h-hole pieces) Cut 2 & work.

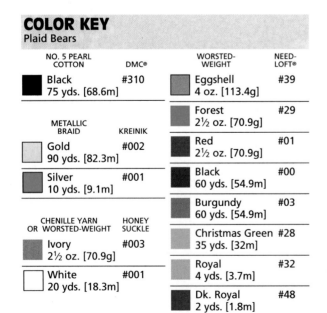

Whipstitch to one O. — Whipstitch to one O.

Whipstitch to one O.

Optional Tissue Cover Bottom Assembly Illustration

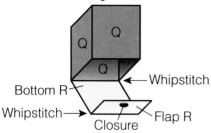

Q
Q
Q

Bottom R
Whipstitch → ← Whipstitch
Closure
Flap R

M – Coaster
(23w x 23h-hole pieces)
Cut 4 & work.

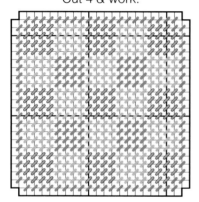

I – Candle Holder Side Support
(35w x 35h-hole pieces)
Cut 3 & work.

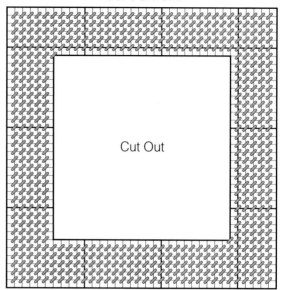

Cut Out

Candle Holder Assembly Diagram
(Pieces are shown in different colors for contrast; gray denotes wrong side.)

Step 1:
Holding one G to each F, with eggshell, whipstitch F & G pieces together & to K, forming Center Assembly; whipstitch J to inside of Assembly.

Step 2:
With black, overcast unfinished edges of F pieces.

Step 3:
Slide I pieces over Center Assembly; with eggshell, whipstitch cutout edges of I to Center Assembly.

Step 4:
With black, whipstitch four H pieces together & to upper two I pieces; whipstitch remaining H pieces together & to K & remaining I piece.

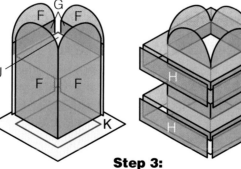

Ho Ho Ho Door Décor

Designed by Virginia and Michael Lamp

Use this familiar greeting to welcome your guests with good cheer.

SIZE: 6½" x 33 ¼" [16.5cm x 84.5cm]

SKILL LEVEL: Average

MATERIALS:
- One 13 ⅝" x 21 ⅝" [34.6cm x 54.9cm] sheet of 7-mesh plastic canvas
- Two ¾" [19mm] gold jingle bells
- Craft glue or glue gun
- Worsted-weight or plastic canvas yarn (for amounts see Color Key)

CUTTING INSTRUCTIONS:
A: For Santa Head, cut one according to graph.
B: For Santa Mustache, cut one according to graph.
C: For Santa Mittens, cut two according to graph.
D: For Banner Pieces #1 and #2, cut one according to graph for Piece #1 and one 21w x 92h-holes for Piece #2 (no #2 graph).
E: For "H's", cut three according to graph.
F: For "O's", cut three according to graph.
G: For Holly Leaves, cut six according to graph.
H: For Holly Berries, cut six according to graph.

STITCHING INSTRUCTIONS:
1: Using colors and stitches indicated, work A-C, D#1 and E-H pieces according to graphs; work D#2 according to pattern established on D#1. With silver for Santa's beard, hat pom-pom and Mustache, cherry red for hat, cornmeal for "H's" and "O's", paddy green for Banner, and with matching colors as shown in photo, overcast cutouts and outer edges of pieces.

2: Using colors (Separate into individual plies if desired.) and embroidery stitches indicated, embroider detail on A as indicated on graph.

3: Glue Santa's Mustache to right side of Santa's Head, Santa's Mittens to wrong side of Santa's Head and Santa's Head to right side of Banner as shown. Evenly space letters on right side of

Banner as desired or as shown and glue to secure; glue bells to bottom of Banner (see photo). Hang as desired.

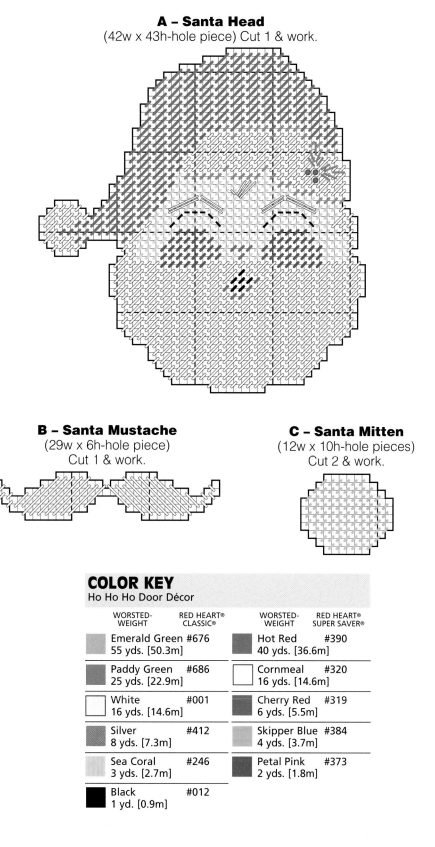

A – Santa Head
(42w x 43h-hole piece) Cut 1 & work.

B – Santa Mustache
(29w x 6h-hole piece)
Cut 1 & work.

C – Santa Mitten
(12w x 10h-hole pieces)
Cut 2 & work.

COLOR KEY
Ho Ho Ho Door Décor

WORSTED-WEIGHT	RED HEART® CLASSIC®	WORSTED-WEIGHT	RED HEART® SUPER SAVER®
Emerald Green #676 55 yds. [50.3m]		Hot Red #390 40 yds. [36.6m]	
Paddy Green #686 25 yds. [22.9m]		Cornmeal #320 16 yds. [14.6m]	
White #001 16 yds. [14.6m]		Cherry Red #319 6 yds. [5.5m]	
Silver #412 8 yds. [7.3m]		Skipper Blue #384 4 yds. [3.7m]	
Sea Coral #246 3 yds. [2.7m]		Petal Pink #373 2 yds. [1.8m]	
Black #012 1 yd. [0.9m]			

E – "H"
(21w x 25h-hole pieces)
Cut 3 & work.

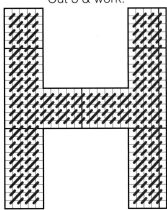

H – Holly Berry
(4w x 4h-hole pieces)
Cut 6 & work.

G – Holly Leaf
(9w x 18h-hole pieces)
Cut 6 & work.

F – "O"
(21w x 25h-hole pieces)
Cut 3 & work.

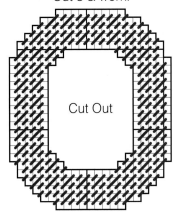

Cut Out

STITCH KEY
| ─ | Backstitch/Straight |
| ● | French Knot |

D – Banner Piece #1
(21w x 92h-hole piece)
Cut 1 & work, overlapping with
D#2 four holes & working
through both thicknesses
at overlap area to join.

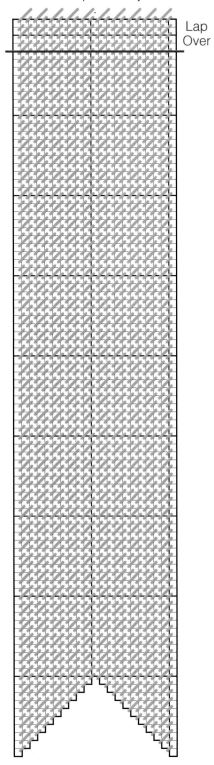

Lap
Over

COLOR KEY
Ho Ho Ho Door Decor

	WORSTED-WEIGHT	RED HEART® CLASSIC®		WORSTED-WEIGHT	RED HEART® SUPER SAVER®
	Emerald Green 55 yds. [50.3m]	#676		Hot Red 40 yds. [36.6m]	#390
	Paddy Green 25 yds. [22.9m]	#686		Cornmeal 16 yds. [14.6m]	#320
	White 16 yds. [14.6m]	#001		Cherry Red 6 yds. [5.5m]	#319
	Silver 8 yds. [7.3m]	#412		Skipper Blue 4 yds. [3.7m]	#384
	Sea Coral 3 yds. [2.7m]	#246		Petal Pink 2 yds. [1.8m]	#373
	Black 1 yd. [0.9m]	#012			

Children's Nativity

Designed by Kristine Loffredo

Display the true meaning of Christmas with this blessed nativity scene.

SIZE: 10½" x 13" [26.7cm x 33cm], not including Holly

SKILL LEVEL: Average

MATERIALS:
- Two sheets of 7-mesh plastic canvas
- Brown doll hair curls
- Nine red 6mm faceted beads
- 11" x 13" [27.9cm x 33cm] piece of ¼"-thick [6mm] cardboard
- Craft glue or glue gun
- Metallic craft cord (for amount see Color Key)
- #16 metallic braid (for amounts see Color Key)
- Worsted-weight or plastic canvas yarn (for amounts see Color Key)

CUTTING INSTRUCTIONS:
A: For Background, cut one according to graph.
B: For Mary, cut one according to graph.
C: For Joseph, cut one according to graph.
D: For Baby Jesus, cut one according to graph.
E: For Star, cut one according to graph.
F: For Holly Leaves, cut three according to graph.

STITCHING INSTRUCTIONS:
1: Using colors and stitches (Leave ½" [13mm] loops on modified turkey work stitches.) indicated, work pieces according to graphs; with matching colors, overcast edges of pieces.

2: Using metallic braid in colors and embroidery stitches indicated, embroider detail on A-E pieces as indicated on graphs.

NOTE: For Backing, using A as a pattern, cut one from cardboard ⅛" [3mm] smaller at all edges.

3: Glue Backing to wrong side of A; glue Mary, Joseph, Baby Jesus, Star and Leaves to right side of Background as shown in photo. Glue three beads to each Holly Leaf as shown.

4: Cut through loops on modified turkey work stitches; trim as desired. Glue one doll hair curl to Joseph for beard and one doll hair curl to Mary for hair (see photo).

F – Holly Leaves
(19w x 19h-hole pieces)
Cut 3 & work.

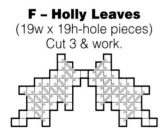

E – Star
(17w x 17h-hole piece)
Cut 1 & work.

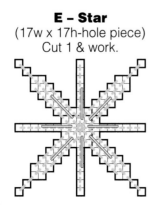

COLOR KEY
Children's Nativity

METALLIC CORD	NEED-LOFT®
Gold 10 yds. [9.1m]	#01

METALLIC BRAID	KREINIK
Chocolate 2 yds. [1.8m]	#201C
Sapphire 2 yds. [1.8m]	#051C
Black 1 yd. [0.9m]	#005C
Gold 1 yd. [0.9m]	#002C

WORSTED-WEIGHT	NEED-LOFT®
Dk. Royal 90 yds. [82.3m]	#48
Gold 25 yds. [22.9m]	#17

WORSTED-WEIGHT	NEED-LOFT®
Cinnamon 15 yds. [13.7m]	#14
Royal 7 yds. [6.4m]	#32
Maple 6 yds. [5.5m]	#13
Baby Blue 5 yds. [4.6m]	#36
Brown 5 yds. [4.6m]	#15
Christmas Green 5 yds. [4.6m]	#28
Orchid 5 yds. [4.6m]	#44
Yellow 5 yds. [4.6m]	#57
Eggshell 2 yds. [1.8m]	#39
Gray 2 yds. [1.8m]	#38

STITCH KEY
- ⊟ Backstitch/Straight
- ● French Knot
- ⊗ Modified Turkey Work

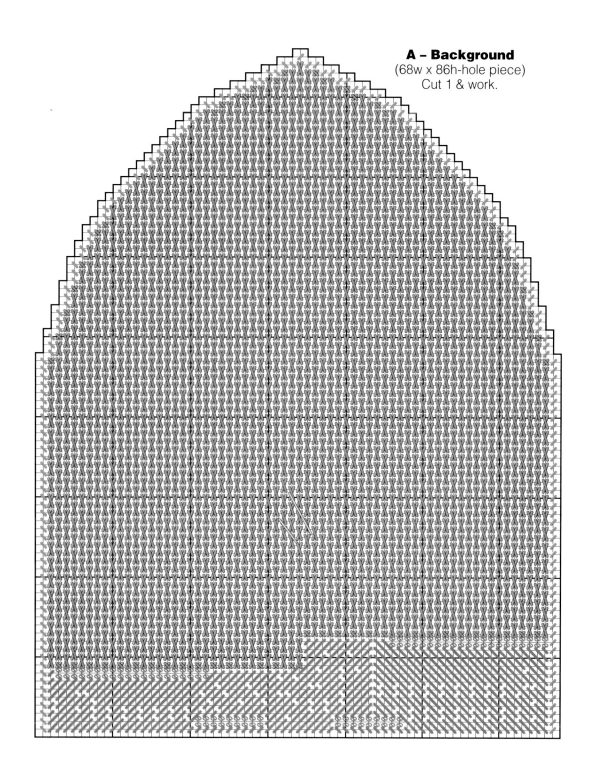

A – Background
(68w x 86h-hole piece)
Cut 1 & work.

B – Mary
(29w x 42h-hole piece)
Cut 1 & work.

C – Joseph
(29w x 54h-hole piece)
Cut 1 & work.

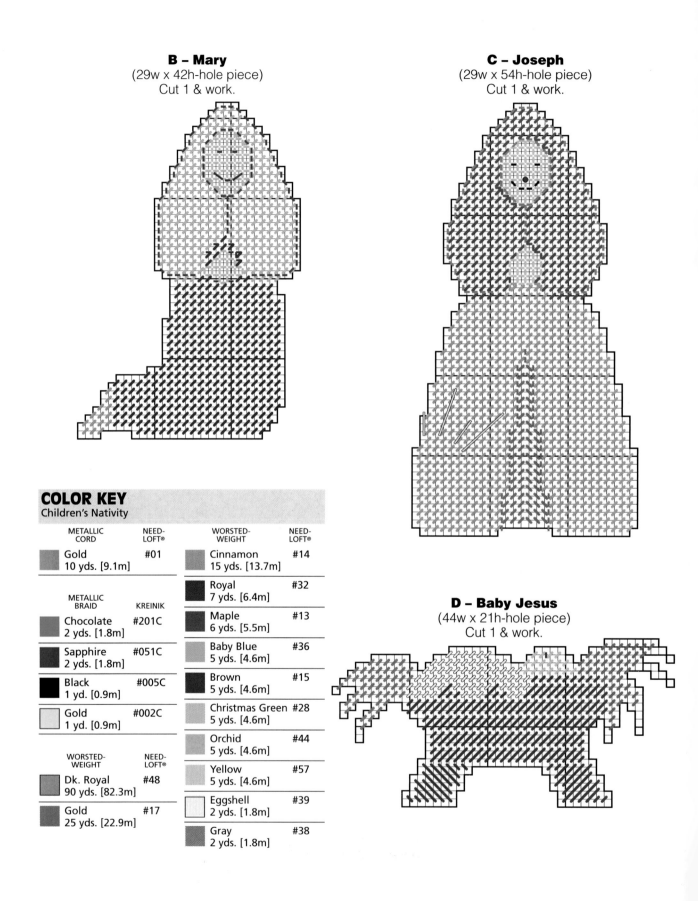

COLOR KEY
Children's Nativity

METALLIC CORD	NEED-LOFT®	WORSTED-WEIGHT	NEED-LOFT®
Gold 10 yds. [9.1m]	#01	Cinnamon 15 yds. [13.7m]	#14
		Royal 7 yds. [6.4m]	#32
METALLIC BRAID	**KREINIK**	Maple 6 yds. [5.5m]	#13
Chocolate 2 yds. [1.8m]	#201C	Baby Blue 5 yds. [4.6m]	#36
Sapphire 2 yds. [1.8m]	#051C	Brown 5 yds. [4.6m]	#15
Black 1 yd. [0.9m]	#005C	Christmas Green 5 yds. [4.6m]	#28
Gold 1 yd. [0.9m]	#002C	Orchid 5 yds. [4.6m]	#44
		Yellow 5 yds. [4.6m]	#57
WORSTED-WEIGHT	**NEED-LOFT®**	Eggshell 2 yds. [1.8m]	#39
Dk. Royal 90 yds. [82.3m]	#48	Gray 2 yds. [1.8m]	#38
Gold 25 yds. [22.9m]	#17		

D – Baby Jesus
(44w x 21h-hole piece)
Cut 1 & work.

Christmas Stocking Pin

Designed by Pam Bull

Brighten your holiday wardrobe with this cute stocking pin.

SIZE: Each is about 1⅜" x 3" long [3.5cm x 7.6cm]

SKILL LEVEL: Challenging

MATERIALS:
- Scrap piece of ivory 14-mesh plastic canvas
- One 1¼" [3.2cm] bar pin
- Craft glue or glue gun
- Six-strand embroidery floss (for amounts see Color Key)

CUTTING INSTRUCTIONS:
A: For Bar, cut one 19w x 5h-holes.
B: For Stockings, cut three according to graph.

STITCHING INSTRUCTIONS:
1: Using colors and stitches indicated, work pieces according to graphs; with med. garnet for Bar and matching colors for Stockings, overcast edges of pieces.

2: Using six strands floss and straight stitch, embroider detail on B pieces as indicated on graph.

3: Cut one each ½" [1.3cm], 1" [2.5cm] and 1½"

[5.1cm] lengths of med. garnet; position and glue one end of each length to wrong side of Bar and remaining end of each length to wrong side of one Stocking as shown in photo.

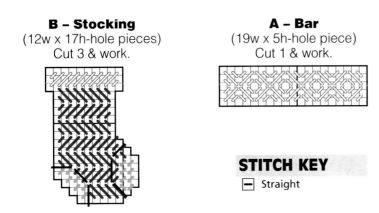

B – Stocking
(12w x 17h-hole pieces)
Cut 3 & work.

A – Bar
(19w x 5h-hole piece)
Cut 1 & work.

STITCH KEY
⊟ Straight

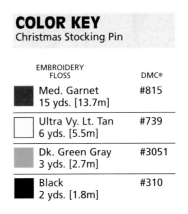

COLOR KEY
Christmas Stocking Pin

	EMBROIDERY FLOSS	DMC®
◼	Med. Garnet 15 yds. [13.7m]	#815
◻	Ultra Vy. Lt. Tan 6 yds. [5.5m]	#739
◼	Dk. Green Gray 3 yds. [2.7m]	#3051
◼	Black 2 yds. [1.8m]	#310

Sparkling Ornament Coasters

Designed by Joan Green

These beautiful ornaments can be displayed on your tree or placed on your holiday table as coasters.

SIZE: Each is 4" x 4⅜" [10.2cm x 11.1cm]

SKILL LEVEL: Easy

MATERIALS:
- One sheet of 7-mesh plastic canvas
- One 9" x 12" [22.9cm x 30.5cm] sheet of gray felt
- Craft glue or glue gun
- Metallic plastic canvas yarn (for amounts see Color Key)

CUTTING INSTRUCTIONS:
A: For Ornament #1, cut one according to graph.
B: For Ornament #2, cut one according to graph.
C: For Ornament #3, cut one according to graph.

D: For Ornament #4, cut one according to graph.
E: For Ornament #5, cut one according to graph.

STITCHING INSTRUCTIONS:
1: Using colors and stitches indicated, work pieces according to graphs; with matching colors as shown in photo, overcast edges of pieces.

2: Using colors and embroidery stitches indicated, embroider detail on B, C and E as indicated on graphs.

3: For Backings, using A-E pieces as patterns, cut one each from felt ⅛" [3mm] smaller at all edges; glue one backing to wrong side of each Ornament Coaster.

A – Ornament #1
(26w x 29h-hole piece)
Cut 1 & work.

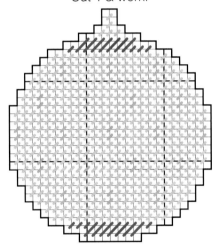

B – Ornament #2
(26w x 29h-hole piece)
Cut 1 & work.

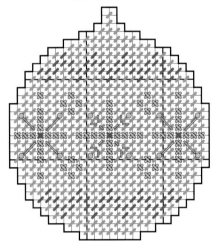

C – Ornament #3
(26w x 29h-hole piece)
Cut 1 & work.

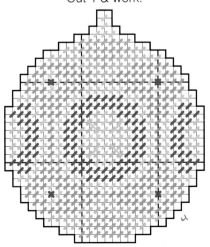

COLOR KEY
Sparkling Ornament Coasters

	METALLIC YARN	RAINBOW GALLERY PC7
	Gold 20 yds. [18.3m]	#01
	Green 15 yds. [13.7m]	#04
	Royal Blue 15 yds. [13.7m]	#06
	Fuchsia 14 yds. [12.8m]	#13
	Purple 8 yds. [7.3m]	#15
	Silver 8 yds. [7.3m]	#02

D – Ornament #4
(26w x 29h-hole piece)
Cut 1 & work.

E – Ornament #5
(26w x 29h-hole piece)
Cut 1 & work.

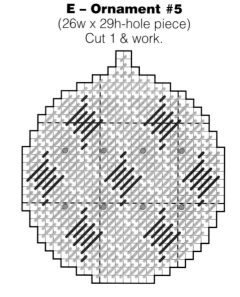

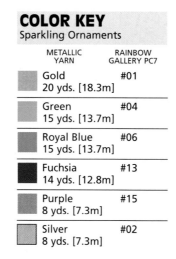

COLOR KEY
Sparkling Ornaments

	METALLIC YARN	RAINBOW GALLERY PC7
	Gold 20 yds. [18.3m]	#01
	Green 15 yds. [13.7m]	#04
	Royal Blue 15 yds. [13.7m]	#06
	Fuchsia 14 yds. [12.8m]	#13
	Purple 8 yds. [7.3m]	#15
	Silver 8 yds. [7.3m]	#02

STITCH KEY
⊟ Backstitch/Straight
⊡ French Knot

St. Nick Ornaments

Designed by Mary Perry

These Old World Santas are perfect gifts for Santa collectors.

SIZE: Each is about 2" x 4¾" [5.1cm x 12.1cm}

SKILL LEVEL: Challenging

MATERIALS:
- One sheet of 10-mesh plastic canvas
- No. 8 pearl cotton (coton perlé) or six-strand embroidery floss (for amount see Color Key)
- #16 medium metallic braid (for amount see Color Key)
- Sport-weight yarn (for amounts see Color Key)

CUTTING INSTRUCTIONS:
A: For Santa Ornament #1 Front and Back, cut one each according to graphs.
B: For Santa Ornament #2 Front and Back, cut one each according to graphs.

STITCHING INSTRUCTIONS:
1: Using colors and stitches indicated, work pieces according to graphs; omitting attachment areas, with matching colors, overcast edges of pieces.

2: Using pearl cotton or three strands floss, yarn (Separate into individual plies, if desired.) and braid in colors and embroidery stitches indicated, embroider detail on pieces as indicated on graphs.

3: With matching colors, whipstitch A pieces wrong sides together as indicated; repeat with B pieces. Hang as desired.

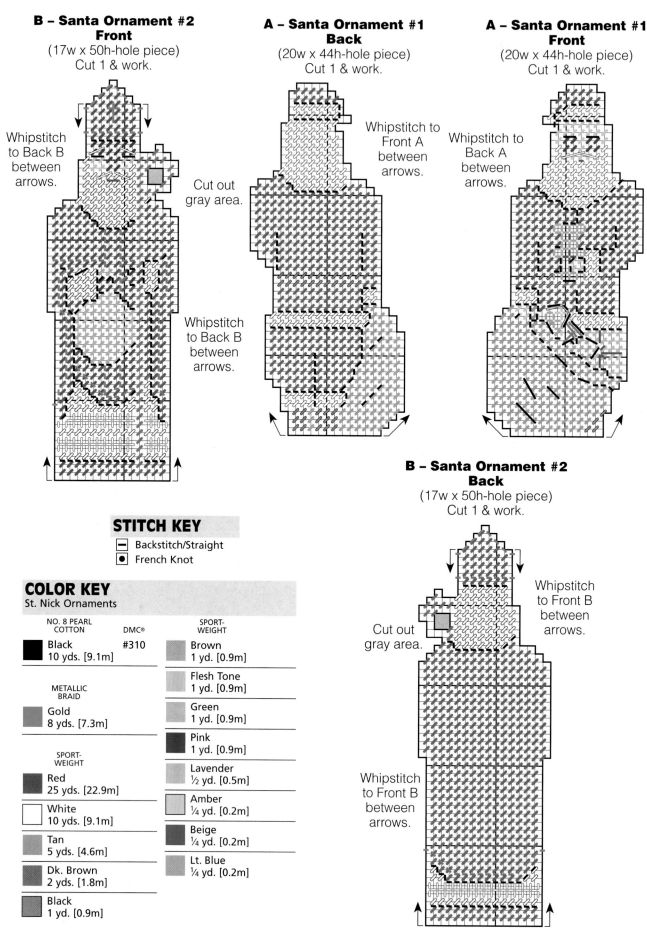

B – Santa Ornament #2 Front
(17w x 50h-hole piece)
Cut 1 & work.

Whipstitch to Back B between arrows.

Cut out gray area.

Whipstitch to Back B between arrows.

A – Santa Ornament #1 Back
(20w x 44h-hole piece)
Cut 1 & work.

Whipstitch to Front A between arrows.

A – Santa Ornament #1 Front
(20w x 44h-hole piece)
Cut 1 & work.

Whipstitch to Back A between arrows.

B – Santa Ornament #2 Back
(17w x 50h-hole piece)
Cut 1 & work.

Cut out gray area.

Whipstitch to Front B between arrows.

Whipstitch to Front B between arrows.

STITCH KEY
- — Backstitch/Straight
- ● French Knot

COLOR KEY
St. Nick Ornaments

NO. 8 PEARL COTTON	DMC®	
Black	#310	
10 yds. [9.1m]		

METALLIC BRAID		
Gold		
8 yds. [7.3m]		

SPORT-WEIGHT		
Red		
25 yds. [22.9m]		
White		
10 yds. [9.1m]		
Tan		
5 yds. [4.6m]		
Dk. Brown		
2 yds. [1.8m]		
Black		
1 yd. [0.9m]		

SPORT-WEIGHT		
Brown		
1 yd. [0.9m]		
Flesh Tone		
1 yd. [0.9m]		
Green		
1 yd. [0.9m]		
Pink		
1 yd. [0.9m]		
Lavender		
½ yd. [0.5m]		
Amber		
¼ yd. [0.2m]		
Beige		
¼ yd. [0.2m]		
Lt. Blue		
¼ yd. [0.2m]		

Package Coasters

Designed by Linda Wyszynski

Guests of all ages will enjoy using these festive coasters.

SIZES: Each Coaster is 3¾" x 3¾" [9.5cm x 9.5cm]; Coaster Holder is 2" x 4¼" x 3¾" tall [5.1cm x 10.8cm x 9.5cm]

SKILL LEVEL: Average

MATERIALS:
- 1½ sheets of 7-mesh plastic canvas
- 8" x 8" [20.3cm x 20.3cm] sheet of 1⁄16" [2mm] corkboard
- Craft glue or glue gun
- Metallic craft cord (for amount see Color Key)
- Worsted-weight or plastic canvas yarn (for amounts see Color Key)

CUTTING INSTRUCTIONS:
A: For Coaster Fronts and Backings, cut 8 (four for Fronts and four for Backings) according to graph.
B: For Coaster Holder Front, cut one according to graph.
C: For Coaster Holder Back, cut one 27w x 17h-holes (no graph).
D: For Coaster Holder Sides, cut two 13w x 17h-holes (no graph).
E: For Coaster Holder Bottom, cut one 27w x 13h-holes (no graph).

STITCHING INSTRUCTIONS:
NOTE: Backing A and E pieces are not worked.

1: Using colors and stitches indicated, work Front A and B pieces according to graphs; work C and D pieces using holly and continental stitch.

NOTE: Cut four 2½" x 3⅝" [6.4cm x 9.2cm] pieces of corkboard.

2: For each Coaster (make 4), holding one Backing A to wrong side of one Front A, with matching colors whipstitch cutouts and outer edges together; glue one piece of corkboard to Coaster Backing.

3: With holly, whipstitch B-E pieces together as indicated, forming Holder; with cord, overcast unfinished edges and cutouts.

B – Coaster Holder Front
(27w x 25h-hole piece)
Cut 1 & work.

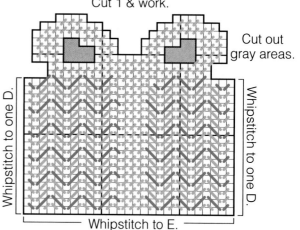

Whipstitch to one D.

Whipstitch to one D.

Cut out gray areas.

Whipstitch to E.

A – Coaster Front and Backing
(25w x 25h-hole pieces)
Cut 8. Work 4 for Fronts &
leave 4 unworked for Backings.

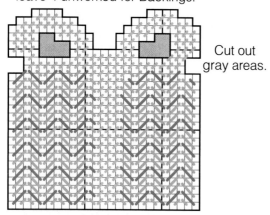

Cut out gray areas.

COLOR KEY
Package Coasters

	METALLIC CORD	NEED-LOFT®
	Gold 20 yds. [18.3m]	#01

	WORSTED-WEIGHT	NEED-LOFT®
	Holly 90 yds. [82.3m]	#27
	Forest 15 yds. [13.7m]	#29
	White 15 yds. [13.7m]	#41

Santa Tissue Cover

Designed by Kimberly A. Suber

Santa is happy to hold your tissues for seasonal sniffles.

SIZE: Snugly covers a boutique-style tissue box

SKILL LEVEL: Average

MATERIALS:
- 1½ sheets of 7-mesh plastic canvas
- Craft glue or glue gun
- Metallic craft cord (for amount see Color Key)
- Worsted-weight or plastic canvas yarn (for amounts see Color Key)

CUTTING INSTRUCTIONS:
A: For Top, cut one according to graph.
B: For Sides, cut four 30w x 36h-holes.

STITCHING INSTRUCTIONS:
1: Using colors and stitches indicated, work pieces according to graphs. Alternating green and white for candy cane effect, overcast cutout edges of A.

2: Using colors (Separate into individual plies, if desired.) and embroidery stitches indicated, embroider detail on B pieces as indicated on graph.

3: Alternating green and white for candy cane effect, whipstitch A and B pieces wrong sides together; overcast unfinished edges.

4: Cut four 9" [22.9cm] lengths of cord; tie each length into a bow. Glue one bow to each Cover Side as shown in photo.

STITCH KEY
- ⊟ Backstitch/Straight
- ⊡ French Knot

COLOR KEY
Santa Tissue Cover

METALLIC CORD		WORSTED-WEIGHT	
Gold 12 yds. [11m]		Dk. Blue 12 yds. [11m]	

WORSTED-WEIGHT			
Lt. Blue 40 yds. [36.6m]		Black 8 yds. [7.3m]	
Dk. Red 30 yds. [27.4m]		Dk. Green 4 yds. [3.7m]	
White 25 yds. [22.9m]		Peach 4 yds. [3.7m]	
Green 15 yds. [13.7m]		Pink 1 yd. [0.9m]	

B – Side
(30w x 36h-hole pieces)
Cut 4 & work, filling in uncoded areas
using lt. blue & continental stitch.

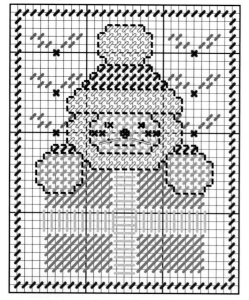

A – Top
(30w x 30h-hole piece)
Cut 1 & work, filling in uncoded areas
using lt. blue & continental stitch.

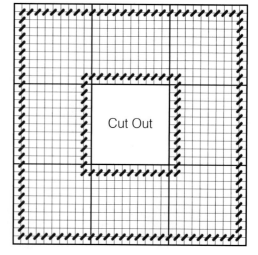

Cut Out

Santa's Key

Designed by Sandra Miller Maxfield

No fireplace? No problem. Invite Santa into your house with this special key.

SIZE: 10⅜" x 13¾" [26.4cm x 34.9cm]

SKILL LEVEL: Average

MATERIALS:
- Two sheets of 7-mesh plastic canvas
- ⅓ yd. [0.3m] emerald ¼" [6mm] satin ribbon
- Craft glue or glue gun
- Metallic craft cord (for amount see Color Key)
- Worsted-weight or plastic canvas yarn (for amounts see Color Key)

CUTTING INSTRUCTIONS:
A: For Background, cut one 69w x 90h-holes.
B: For Key, cut one according to graph.

STITCHING INSTRUCTIONS:
1: Using colors and stitches indicated, work pieces according to graphs; with black for Background and with matching colors, overcast edges of pieces.

STITCH KEY
- ⊟ Backstitch/Straight
- ⊙ French Knot

COLOR KEY
Santa's Key

METALLIC CORD		WORSTED-WEIGHT		WORSTED-WEIGHT	
▦	Gold 8 yds. [7.3m]	▪	Red 4 yds. [3.7m]	▨	Yellow 3 yds. [2.7m]
WORSTED-WEIGHT		▪	Christmas Red 3 yds. [2.7m]	▨	Lt. Pink 2 yds. [1.8m]
☐	White 67 yds. [61.3m]	▪	Green 3 yds. [2.7m]	▨	Gray 1 yd. [0.9m]
▨	Lt. Blue 30 yds. [27.4m]	▪	Purple 3 yds. [2.7m]	▪	Lavender 1 yd. [0.9m]
■	Black 15 yds. [13.7m]	▪	Royal 3 yds. [2.7m]		

2: Using colors (Separate into individual plies if desired.) and embroidery stitches indicated, embroider detail on A (for name, use letters of choice according to Alphabet Graph) and B pieces as indicated on graphs.

3: Tie ribbon into a bow; glue to top of Key as shown in photo. Glue Key to Background as shown; hang as desired.

Cut out gray area.

B – Key
(28w x 80h-hole piece)
Cut 1 & work.

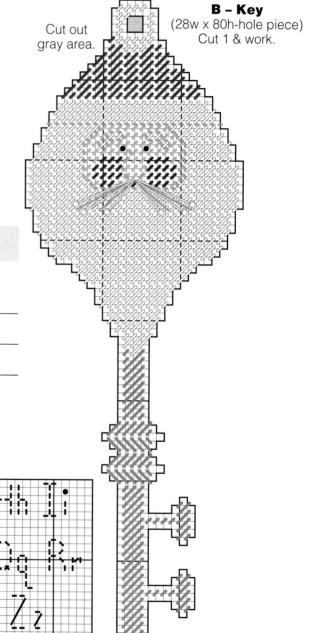

Alphabet Graph

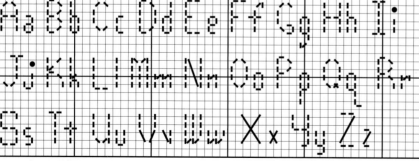

A – Background (69w x 90h-hole piece)
Cut 1 & work, filling in uncoded areas using white & continental stitch

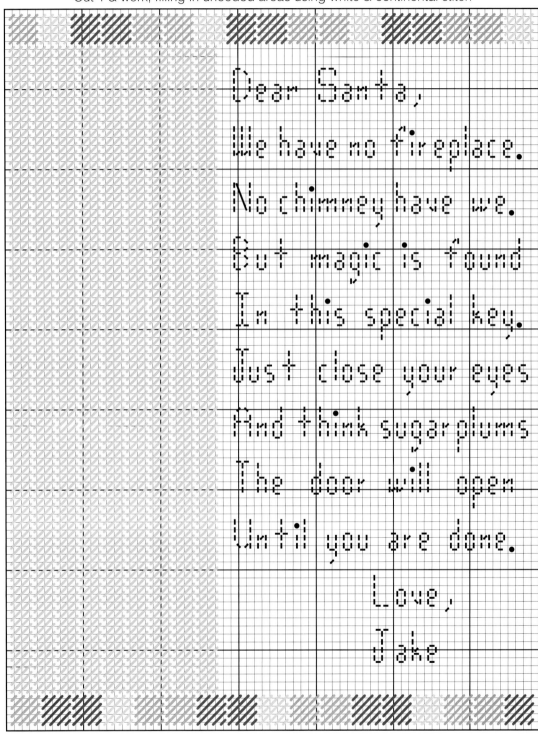

Dear Santa,
We have no fireplace.
No chimney have we.
But magic is found
In this special key.
Just close your eyes
And think sugarplums
The door will open
Until you are done.
Love,
Jake

Candy Cane Holders

Designed by Debbie Tabor

These merry characters bear sweet treats for festive party favors.

SIZES: Santa is ¾" x 5" x 5¼" [1.9cm x 12.7cm x 13.3cm], not including hanger or candy cane; Reindeer is ¾" x 5 x 5½" [1.9cm x 12.7cm x 14cm], not including hanger or candy cane

SKILL LEVEL: Average

MATERIALS:
• One sheet of 7-mesh plastic canvas
• Two candy canes
• Worsted-weight or plastic canvas yarn (for amounts see Color Key)

CUTTING INSTRUCTIONS:
A: For Santa, cut one according to graph.
B: For Santa Mittens #1 and #2, cut one each according to graphs.
C: For Reindeer, cut one according to graph.
D: For Reindeer Hooves, cut two according to graph.

STITCHING INSTRUCTIONS:
1: Using colors and stitches indicated, work pieces according to graphs; do not overcast edges of pieces.

2: Using six strands floss in colors and embroidery stitches indicated, embroider detail on pieces as indicated on graphs.

3: Using black floss for mittens and white floss for hoofs, tack B pieces to A and D pieces to C as indicated; insert candy cane in Holder as shown in photo. Hang or display as desired.

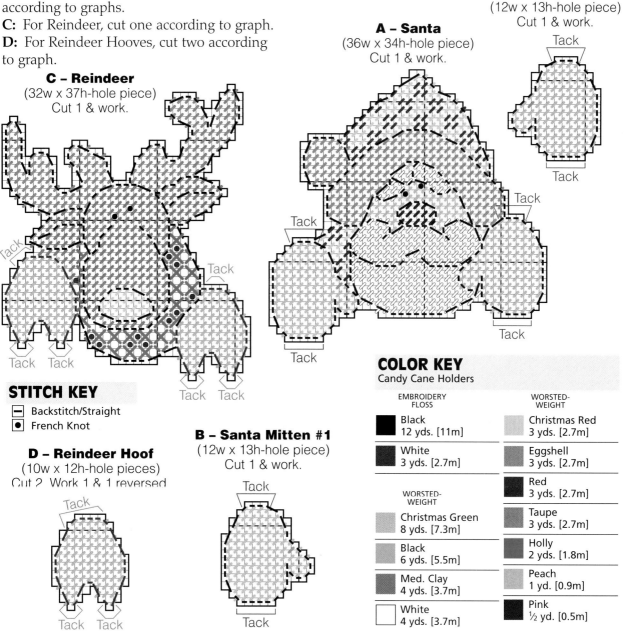

B – Santa Mitten #2
(12w x 13h-hole piece)
Cut 1 & work.
Tack
Tack

A – Santa
(36w x 34h-hole piece)
Cut 1 & work.
Tack
Tack
Tack

C – Reindeer
(32w x 37h-hole piece)
Cut 1 & work.
Tack
Tack
Tack Tack
Tack Tack

STITCH KEY
– Backstitch/Straight
• French Knot

D – Reindeer Hoof
(10w x 12h-hole pieces)
Cut 2, Work 1 & 1 reversed
Tack
Tack Tack

B – Santa Mitten #1
(12w x 13h-hole piece)
Cut 1 & work.
Tack
Tack

COLOR KEY
Candy Cane Holders

EMBROIDERY FLOSS		WORSTED-WEIGHT	
■ Black 12 yds. [11m]		Christmas Red 3 yds. [2.7m]	
■ White 3 yds. [2.7m]		Eggshell 3 yds. [2.7m]	
WORSTED-WEIGHT		Red 3 yds. [2.7m]	
Christmas Green 8 yds. [7.3m]		Taupe 3 yds. [2.7m]	
Black 6 yds. [5.5m]		Holly 2 yds. [1.8m]	
Med. Clay 4 yds. [3.7m]		Peach 1 yd. [0.9m]	
□ White 4 yds. [3.7m]		Pink ½ yd. [0.5m]	

Kwanzaa!

*C*elebrate this great African-American holiday
with a Kinara which is symbolic of African roots,
their parent people and continental Africans.

Kinara Kwanzaa With Frame

Designed by Mary Perry

Remember the special African-American festival with this symbolic frame.

SIZE: 3" x 7¼" x 6" tall [7.6cm x 18.4cm x 15.2cm] with a 3⅝" x 4¾" [9.2cm x 12.1cm] photo window

MATERIALS:
- 1½ sheets of 7-mesh plastic canvas
- Heavy metallic braid (for amount see Color Key)
- Raffia or satin straw (for amount see Color Key)
- Worsted-weight or plastic canvas yarn (for amounts see Color Key)

CUTTING INSTRUCTIONS:
A: For Front, cut one 47w x 39h-holes.
B: For Frame Front, cut one according to graph.
C: For Frame Backing, cut one according to graph.
D: For Frame Supports, cut two according to graph.

STITCHING INSTRUCTIONS:
NOTE: C is not worked.

1: Using colors indicated and continental stitch, work A, B and D pieces according to graphs; with med. blue, overcast cutout edges of B.

2: Using yarn (Separate into individual plies if desired.) and embroidery stitches indicated, embroider detail on A as indicated on graph.

3: For Frame, with med. blue, whipstitch C to wrong side of B as indicated on graph; with silver, whipstitch top edge of Frame to A as indicated through all thicknesses.

4: With silver, overcast unfinished edges of A, attaching D pieces to A as indicated as you work; with med. blue, overcast all unfinished edges.

A – Front
(47w x 39h-hole piece) Cut 1 & work.

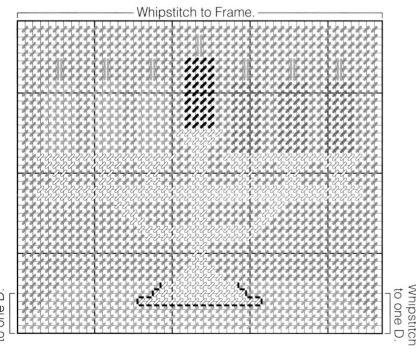

Whipstitch to Frame.

Whipstitch to one D.

Whipstitch to one D.

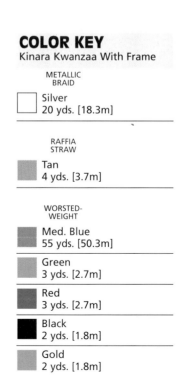

COLOR KEY
Kinara Kwanzaa With Frame

METALLIC BRAID

Silver
20 yds. [18.3m]

RAFFIA STRAW

Tan
4 yds. [3.7m]

WORSTED-WEIGHT

Med. Blue
55 yds. [50.3m]

Green
3 yds. [2.7m]

Red
3 yds. [2.7m]

Black
2 yds. [1.8m]

Gold
2 yds. [1.8m]

B – Frame Front
(47w x 39h-hole piece) Cut 1 & work.

Whipstitch to A & C.

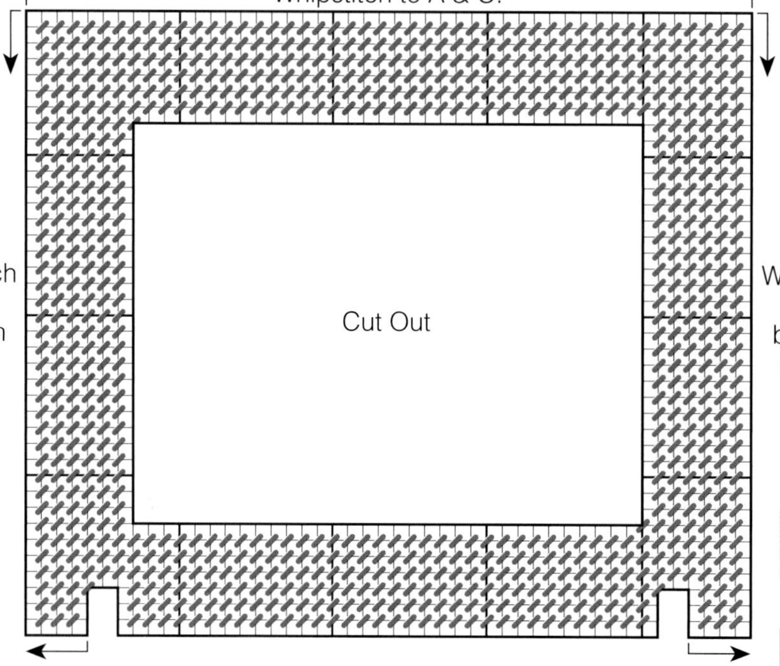

Whipstitch to C between arrows.

Cut Out

Whipstitch to C between arrows.

D – Frame Support
(20w x 5h-hole pieces)
Cut 2. Work 1 & 1 reversed.

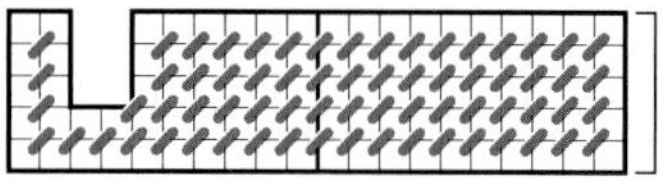

Whipstitch to A.

STITCH KEY

⊟ Backstitch/Straight

C – Frame Backing
(47w x 39h-hole piece) Cut 1 & work.

Whipstitch to A & B.

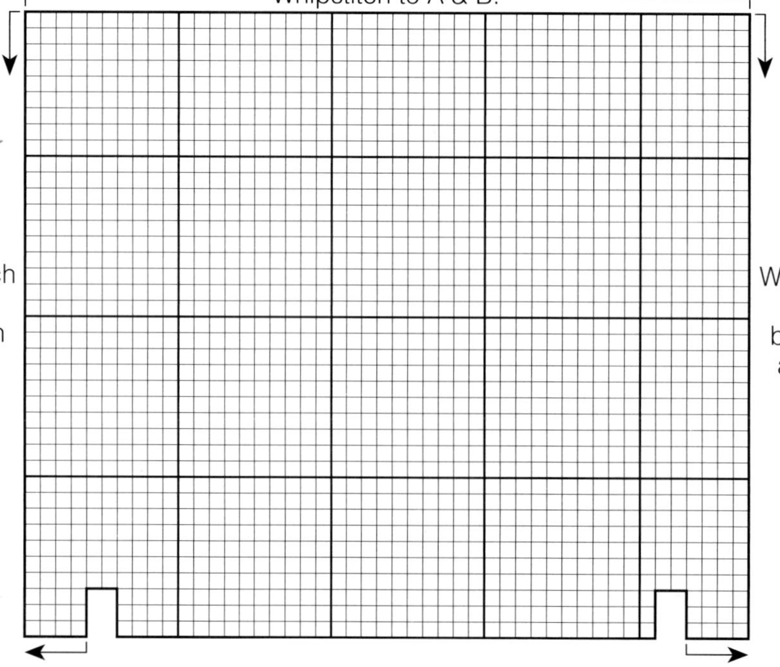

Whipstitch to B between arrows.

Whipstitch to B between arrows.

COLOR KEY
Kinara Kwanzaa With Frame

METALLIC BRAID

☐ Silver
20 yds. [18.3m]

RAFFIA STRAW

Tan
4 yds. [3.7m]

WORSTED-WEIGHT

Med. Blue
55 yds. [50.3m]

Green
3 yds. [2.7m]

Red
3 yds. [2.7m]

Black
2 yds. [1.8m]

Gold
2 yds. [1.8m]

Ready, Set, Stitch

*Get ready to stitch like a pro
with these simple, step-by-step guidelines.*

GETTING STARTED

Most plastic canvas stitchers love getting their projects organized before they even step out the door in search of supplies. A few moments of careful planning can make the creation of your project even more fun.

First of all, prepare your work area. You will need a flat surface for cutting and assembly, and you will need a place to store your materials. Good lighting is essential, and a comfortable chair will make your stitching time even more enjoyable.

Do you plan to make one project, or will you be making several of the same item? A materials list appears at the beginning of each pattern. If you plan to make several of the same item, multiply your materials accordingly. Your shopping list is ready.

CHOOSING CANVAS

Most projects can be made using standard-size sheets of canvas. Standard size sheets of 7-mesh (7 holes per inch) are always 70 x 90 holes and are about 10½" x 13½" [26.7cm x 34.3cm]. For larger projects, 7-mesh canvas also comes in 12" x 18" [30.5cm x 45.7cm],

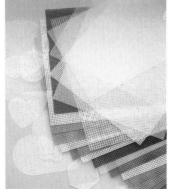

which is always 80 x 120 holes and 13½" x 22½" [34.3cm x 57.2cm], which is always 90 x 150 holes. Other shapes are available in 7-mesh, including circles, diamonds, purse forms and ovals.

10-mesh canvas (10 holes per inch) comes only in standard-size sheets, which vary slightly depending on brand. They are 10½" x 13½" [26.7cm x 34.3cm], which is always 106 x 136 holes or 11" x 14" [27.9cm x 35.6cm], which is always 108 x 138 holes.

5-mesh canvas (5 holes per inch) and 14-mesh (14 holes per inch) sheets are also available.

Some canvas is soft and pliable, while other canvas is stiffer and more rigid. To prevent canvas from cracking during or after stitching, you'll want to choose pliable canvas for projects that require shaping, like round baskets with curved handles. For easier shaping, warm canvas pieces with a blow-dry hair dryer to soften; dip in cool water to set. If your project is a box or an item that will stand alone, stiffer canvas is more suitable.

Both 7- and 10-mesh canvas sheets are available in a rainbow of colors. Most designs can be stitched on colored as well as clear canvas. When a pattern does not specify color in the materials list, you can assume clear canvas was used in the photographed model. If you'd like to stitch only a portion of the design, leaving a portion unstitched, use colored canvas to coordinate with yarn colors.

Buy the same brand of canvas for each entire project. Different brands of canvas may differ slightly in the distance between each bar.

MARKING & COUNTING TOOLS

To avoid wasting canvas, careful cutting of each piece is important. For some pieces with square corners, you might be comfortable cutting the canvas without marking it beforehand. But for pieces with lots of angles and cutouts, you may want to mark your canvas before cutting.

Always count before you mark and cut. To count holes on the graphs, look for the bolder lines showing each ten holes. These ten-count lines begin in the lower left-hand corner of each graph and are on the graph to make counting easier. To count holes on the canvas, you may use your tapestry needle, a toothpick or a plastic hair roller pick. Insert the needle or pick slightly in each hole as you count.

Most stitchers have tried a variety of marking tools and have settled on a favorite, which may be crayon, permanent marker, grease pencil or ball point pen. One of the best marking tools is a fine-point overhead projection marker, available at office supply stores. The ink is dark and easy to see and washes off completely with water. After cutting and before stitching, it's important to remove all marks so they won't stain yarn as you stitch or show through stitches later. Cloth and paper toweling removes grease pencil and crayon marks, as do fabric softener sheets that have already been used in your dryer.

CUTTING TOOLS

You may find it helpful to have several tools on hand for cutting canvas. When cutting long, straight sections, scissors, craft cutters or kitchen shears are the fastest and easiest to use. For cutting out detailed areas and trimming nubs, you may like using manicure scissors or nail clippers. If you prefer laying your canvas flat when cutting, try a craft knife and cutting surface—self-healing mats designed for sewing and kitchen cutting boards work well.

STITCHING MATERIALS

You may choose two-ply nylon plastic canvas yarn or four-ply worsted-weight yarn for stitching on 7-mesh canvas. There are about 42 yards per ounce of plastic canvas yarn and 50 yards per ounce of worsted-weight yarn.

Worsted-weight yarn is widely available and comes in wool, acrylic, cotton and blends. If you decide to use worsted-weight yarn, choose 100% acrylic for best coverage. Select worsted-weight yarn by color instead of the color names or numbers found in the Color Keys. Projects stitched with worsted-weight yarn often "fuzz" after use. "Fuzz" can be removed by shaving it off with a fabric shaver to make your project look new again.

Plastic canvas yarn comes in about 60 colors and is a favorite of many plastic canvas designers. These yarns "wear" well both while stitching and in the finished product. When buying plastic canvas yarn, shop using the color names or numbers found in the Color Keys, or select colors of your choice.

To cover 5-mesh canvas, use a doubled strand of worsted-weight or plastic canvas yarn.

Choose sport-weight yarn or #3 pearl cotton for stitching on 10-mesh canvas. To cover 10-mesh canvas using six-strand embroidery floss, use 12 strands held together. Single and double plies of yarn will also cover 10-mesh and can be used for embroidery or accent stitching worked over needlepoint stitches —simply separate worsted-weight yarn into 2-ply or plastic canvas yarn into 1-ply. Nylon plastic canvas yarn does not perform as well as knitting worsted when separated and can be frustrating to use, but it is possible. Just use short lengths, separate into single plies and twist each ply slightly.

Embroidery floss or #5 pearl cotton can also be used for embroidery, and each covers 14-mesh canvas well.

Metallic cord is a tightly-woven cord that comes in dozens of glittering colors. Some are solid-color metallics, including gold and silver, and some have colors interwoven with gold or silver threads. If your metallic cord has a white core, the core may be removed for super-easy stitching. To do so, cut a length of cord; grasp center core fibers with tweezers or fingertips and pull. Core slips out easily. Though the sparkly look of metallics will add much to your project, you may substitute contrasting colors of yarn.

Natural and synthetic raffia straw will cover 7-mesh canvas if flattened before stitching. Use short lengths to prevent splitting, and glue ends to prevent unraveling.

CUTTING CANVAS

Follow all Cutting Instructions, Notes and labels above graphs to cut canvas. Each piece is labeled with a letter of the alphabet. Square-sided pieces are cut according to hole count, and some may not have a graph.

Unlike sewing patterns, graphs are not designed to be used as actual patterns but rather as counting, cutting and stitching guides. Therefore, graphs may not be actual size. Count the holes on the graph (see Marking & Counting Tools), mark your canvas to match, then cut. The old carpenters' adage—"Measure twice, cut once"—is good advice. Trim off the nubs close to the bar, and trim all corners diagonally.

For large projects, as you cut each piece, it is a good idea to label it with its letter and name. Use sticky labels, or fasten scrap paper notes through the canvas with a twist tie or a quick stitch with a scrap of yarn. To stay organized, you many want to store corresponding pieces together in zip-close bags.

If you want to make several of a favorite design to give as gifts or sell at bazaars, make cutting canvas easier and faster by making a master pattern. From colored canvas, cut out one of each piece required. For duplicates, place the colored canvas on top of clear canvas and cut out. If needed, secure the canvas pieces together with paper fasteners, twist ties or yarn. By using this method, you only have to count from the graphs once.

If you accidentally cut or tear a bar or two on your canvas, don't worry! Boo-boos can usually be repaired in one of several ways: heat the tip of a metal skewer and melt the canvas back together; glue torn bars with a tiny drop of craft glue, super glue or hot glue; or reinforce the torn section with a separate piece of canvas placed at the back of your work. When reinforcing with extra canvas, stitch through both thicknesses.

SUPPLIES

Yarn, canvas, needles, cutters and most other supplies needed to complete the projects in this book are available at craft and needlework stores and through mail order catalogs. Other supplies are available at fabric, hardware and discount stores.

NEEDLES & OTHER STITCHING TOOLS

Blunt-end tapestry needles are used for stitching plastic canvas. Choose a No. 16 needle for stitching 5- and 7-mesh, a No. 18 for stitching 10-mesh and a No. 24 for stitching 14-mesh canvas. A small pair of embroidery scissors for snipping yarn is handy. Try using needle-nosed jewelry pliers for pulling the needle through several thicknesses of canvas and out of tight spots too small for your hand.

STITCHING THE CANVAS

Stitching Instructions for each section are found after the Cutting Instructions. First, refer to the illustrations of basic stitches found on page 159 to familiarize yourself with the stitches used. Illustrations will be found near the graphs for pieces worked using special stitches. Follow the numbers on the tiny graph beside the illustration to make

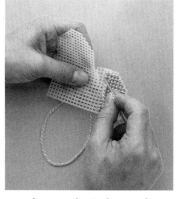

each stitch—bring your needle up from the back of the work on odd numbers and down through the front of the work on the even numbers.

Before beginning, read the Stitching Instructions to get an overview of what you'll be doing. You'll find that some pieces are stitched using colors and stitches indicated on graphs, and for other pieces you will be given a color and stitch to use to cover the entire piece.

Cut yarn lengths between 18" [45.7cm] to 36" [91.4cm]. Thread needle; do not tie a knot in the end. Bring your needle up through the canvas from the back, leaving a short length of yarn on the wrong side of the canvas. As you begin to stitch, work over this short length of yarn. If you are beginning with Continental Stitches, leave a 1" [2.5cm] length, but if you are working longer stitches, leave a longer length.

In order for graph colors to contrast well, graph colors may not match yarn colors. For instance, a light yellow may be selected to represent the metallic cord color gold, or a light blue may represent white yarn.

When following a graph showing several colors, you may want to work all the stitches of one color at the same time. Some stitchers prefer to work with several colors at once by threading each on a separate needle and letting the yarn not being used hang on the wrong side of the work. Either way, remember that strands of yarn run across the wrong side of the work may show through the stitches from the front.

As you stitch, try to maintain an even tension on the yarn. Loose stitches will look uneven, and tight stitches will let the canvas show through. If your yarn twists as you work, you may want to let your needle and yarn hang and untwist occasionally.

When you end a section of stitching or finish a thread, weave the yarn through the back side of your last few stitches; then trim it off.

CONSTRUCTION & ASSEMBLY

After all pieces of an item needing assembly are stitched, you will find the order of assembly is listed in the Stitching Instructions and sometimes illustrated in Diagrams found with the graphs. For best results, join pieces in the order written. Refer to the Stitch Key and to the directives near the graphs for precise attachments.

FINISHING TIPS

To combat glue strings when using a hot glue gun, practice a swirling motion as you work. After placing the drop of glue on your work, lift the gun slightly and swirl to break the stream of glue, as if you were making an ice cream cone. Have a cup of water handy when gluing. For those times that you'll need to touch the glue, first dip your finger into the water just enough to dampen it. This will minimize the glue sticking to your finger, and it will cool and set the glue more quickly.

To attach beads, use a bit more glue to form a cup around the bead. If too much shows after drying, use a craft knife to trim off excess glue.

Scotchguard® or other fabric protectors may be used on your finished projects. However, avoid using a permanent marker if you plan to use a fabric protector, and be sure to remove all other markings before stitching. Fabric protectors can cause markings to bleed, staining yarn.

FOR MORE INFORMATION

Sometimes even the most experienced needlecrafters can find themselves having trouble following instructions. If you have difficulty completing your project, write to Plastic Canvas Editors, The Needlecraft Shop, 23 Old Pecan Road, Big Sandy, TX 75755 (903) 636-4000 or (800) 259-4000, www.needle-craftshop.com.

Stitch Guide

Continental

Continental Reverse

Cross

Long Over Three Bars

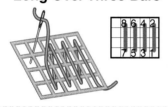

Diagonal Horizontal

Diagonal Vertical

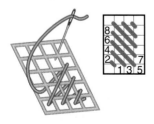

Modified Turkey Work

Overcast

Smyrna Cross

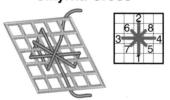

Whipstitch

Diagonal Reverse Horizontal

Diagonal Reverse Vertical

Herringbone Overcast

Herringbone Whipstitch

Mosiac

Scotch Over Three Bars

Reverse Scotch

Alternate Scotch

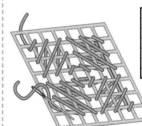

Backstitch

Bead Attachment

French Knot

Lazy Daisy Stitch

Straight

Acknowledgments

Anchor®
• Pearl cotton

Artistic Wire Ltd™
• 18-gauge wire in lemon, rose, silver and green.

Beacon™
• Fabri-Tac™ Permanent Adhesive

Coats & Clark
• Red Heart® Yarn

DMC®
• Floss
• Pearl Cotton

Daniel Enterprises
• Stitch-A-Mug

Darice®
• 7 and 10 mesh clear plastic canvas
• Pearlized metallic cord
• Crystal E Beads #1102-84
• Silver windchimes #1624-30
• 4mm x 7mm silver chain #18635
• 7mm silver jump ring #1881-10
• 10mm silver jump rings #1881-12

• ¾" bone ring #10122
• 13mm x 8mm lavender #0622-27 and lt. blue #0622-27 pear shaped acrylic rhinestones
• 5mm lavender, lt. blue, pink, and amethyst round acrylic rhinestones #1811-16
• 3mm moveable eyes #ME 3/PP
• 4mm moveable eyes #ME 4/PP
• 31mm x 31mm crystal acrylic hearts #0639-27
• Floral stake #WP-12-GPP
• 26-gauge black wire #3204-05
• Glass votive candle holder #1015-88
• Tea candle #1010-21
• 16-gauge green stem wire #32050-1
• 4" butterfly antennaes #3205-05

Elmore-Pisgah, Inc.
• Chenille Yarn

Kreinik
• ⅛" metallic ribbon
• #32 metallic braid
• #16 metallic braid

Kunin
• PrestoFelt®

Le Bouton
• ⅛" white buttons

Offray
• #580 emerald ribbon

Rainbow Gallery®
• Plastic canvas yarn
• Metallic PC7 yarn

Soft Flex®
• Soft Touch™ beading wire

Streamline
• 5/16" white buttons

Uniek
• QuickCount® 7-mesh plastic canvas in clear, white, black and orange
• Plastic canvas shapes
• Needloft® plastic canvas yarn
• Needloft® metallic cord

Westrim
• Animal nose
• Animal eyes

Yarn Tree Designs
• 14-count metallic gold perforated paper

Pattern Index

Designer Index